SECRET CODES 2001 v.2

PlayStation®

PlayStation®2

Dreamcast®

Nintendo 64®

Game Boy®

//////BRADYGAMES

TAKE YOUR GAME FURTHER™

SECRET CODES 2001 V.2

LEGAL STUFF

Brady Publishing
An Imprint of Pearson Education
201 W. 103rd St.
Indianapolis, IN 46290

ISBN: 0-7440-0076-9
Library of Congress Catalog No.: 2001 135082

Printing Code: The rightmost double-digit number is the year of the book's printing; the rightmost single-digit number is the number of the book's printing. For example, 00-1 shows that the first printing of the book occurred in 2000.

04 03 02 01
4 3 2 1

TABLE OF CONTENTS

BRADYGAMES STAFF

Director of Publishing
David Waybright

Editor-In-Chief
H. Leigh Davis

Marketing Manager
Janet Eshenour

Creative Director
Robin Lasek

Licensing Assistant
Mike Degler

Marketing Assistant
Susie Nieman

CREDITS

Project Editor
Christian Sumner

Screenshot Editor
Michael Owen

Book Designer
Kurt Owens

Production Designers
Jane Washburne
Bob Klunder
Tracy Wehmeyer

THE GAMES

PLAYSTATION®

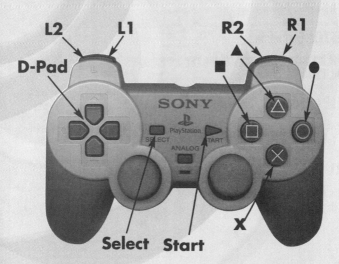

007 RACING

ASTON MARTIN VANTAGE IN TWO-PLAYER

At the title screen, press L1, R1, ▲, ●, ✕. You'll hear a sound if the codes was entered correctly.

40 WINKS

BIG HEAD

Pause the game, press and hold the Select button, and then press L1, Up, Right, L2, Up and release the Select button. Then hold the Select button and press L1, Up, Right, L2, Up.

ALL DREAMKEYS

At the House Hub, press ●, L1, L2, L1, L2.

ALL WINKS

At the House Hub, press Left, Down, Right, Right, Right.

RESET ZS

Pause the game, press and hold the Select button, and then press Right, L1, Up, R1, L1.

RESTORE LIVES

Pause the game, press and hold the Select button, and then press L1, Up, Right, L2, Up.

RESET MOONS

Pause the game, press and hold the Select button, and then press Up, L2, Left, R2, Left.

FILL COGS

Pause the game, press and hold the Select button, and then press Down, R2, L1, Up, R2.

APE ESCAPE

COLLECT UP TO 99 EXPLOSIVE BULLETS

Pause the game and press R2, Down, L2, Up, Right, Down, Right, Left.

ARMY MEN: AIR ATTACK 2

PASSWORDS

MISSION	PASSWORD

Enter Password   Mission 22

2	Up, X, ▲, Right, Left, ■, ●. X
3	▲, ●, Down, Left, ■, ■, Up, Up
4	X, Right, Left, X, ●, ■, ■, ▲
5	Down, Down, ●, ■, ●, ■, Right, X
6	▲, X, Up, Left, Right, Left, ●, ▲
7	Left, ■, Right, Down, ●, X, X, Right
8	▲, Right, ■, ■, ●, Down, Down, X
9	Up, X, ■, Left, Right, ●, Left, Left
10	▲, Up, ●, X, ■, Down, Down, Down
11	●, ●, Up, Left, Right, X, ▲, ■
13	Left, Left, ▲, ●, X, X, Down, Right
15	Left, Right, ●, X, ■, Down, Down, ●
16	▲, ●, X, Right, Right, ●, ■, Down
18	●, X, Right, ▲, ■, Up, X, X
20	Up, X, ●, Up, Left, ■, ●, X
21	Left, ●, ▲, Down, X, X, X, ●
22	▲, X, Down, Left, Right, X, ●, ■

BEAST WARS: TRANSFORMERS

LEVEL SKIP

Pause the game. Hold L2 and press Up, Down, Left, Right, ▲, X, X, ▲, Right, Left, Down, Up, Start.

POWER UP WEAPONS

Pause the game. Hold L2 and press Up, Down, Left, Right, ▲, X, ■, Start.

BLADE

While at the main menu, enter these following combinations to access the Cheat Menu located in the in-game menu:

Cheat Menu

INFINITE WEAPONS

Down, Right, Up, Left, L2, L1, R2, R1

UNLIMITED HEALTH

Left, Left, Left, Right, L2, L1, R2, R1.

ALL ITEMS

Right, Left, Up, Down, L2, L2, R2, R2.

All Items

CLOCK TOWER 2: THE STRUGGLE WITHIN

SPECIAL POWER CHARM

At the Title screen, hold L1 + R1 + L2 + R2 while starting a new game.

ALTERNATE OUTFIT

At the Title screen, hold L1 + R2 + Select + ▲ while starting a new game.

Alyssa: "What was that?"

Alternate Outfit

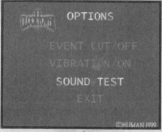

Sound Test

SOUND TEST

At the Title screen, press Left, ●, Down, ▲, Right, ■, Up, ✖, L1, R2, L2, R1 + Start. You'll find the Sound Test option at the Options screen.

COLIN MCRAE RALLY 2.0

CODES

Create a new driver with the following names:

CODE	EFFECT
EASYROLLER	Big wheels
RUBBERTREES	Soft collision
FRIDAYSCHILD	No damage
PRUNEJUICE	Faster game
GREATBALLSOF	Fireballs—Use Handbrake to shoot
ROCKETFUEL	Turbo
NEURALNIGHTMARE	Better AI
MOONLANDER	Low gravity
OFFROAD	Lancer Road Car

continued

CODE	EFFECT
JOBINITALY	Mini Cooper Car
JIMMYSCAR	Sierra Cosworth Car
COOLESTCAR	Ford Puma Car
HELLOCLEVELAND	All Tracks
ONECAREFULOWNER	All Cars
RORRIMSKCART	Mirrored tracks

COLONY WARS 3: RED SUN

CHEAT CODE SCREEN

At the Home Station screen, press R2, R2, L2, L2, R1, R1, Select, Select.

ALL WEAPONS

Enter **Armoury** as a code.

CTR (CRASH TEAM RACING)

RACE AS PENTA PENGUIN

At the Main Menu, press and hold L1 +
R1 and press Down, Right, ▲, Down,
Left, ▲, and Up. You'll hear a sound
when entered correctly. You can race as
Penta Penguin in all modes except
Adventure mode.

Penta Penguin

RACE AS KOMODO JOE

At the Main Menu, press and hold L1 + R1 and press Down, ●, Left, Left, ▲,
Right, and Down. You'll hear a sound when entered correctly. You can race as
Komodo Joe in all modes except Adventure mode.

RACE AS DR. N. TROPHY

At the Main Menu, press and hold L1 + R1 and press Down, Left, Right, Up,
Down, Right, and Right. You'll hear a sound when entered correctly. You can race
as Dr. N. Trophy in all modes except Adventure mode.

RACE AS PAPU PAPU

At the Main Menu, press and hold L1 + R1 and press Left, ▲, Right, Down, Right, ●, Left, Left, and Down. You'll hear a sound when entered correctly. You can race as Papu Papu in all modes except Adventure mode.

RACE AS PINSTRIPE

At the Main Menu, press and hold L1 + R1 and press Left, Right, ▲, Down, Right, and Down. You'll hear a sound when entered correctly. You can race as Pinstripe in all modes except Adventure mode.

Race as Pinstripe

RACE AS RIPPER ROO

At the Main Menu, press and hold L1 + R1 and press Right, ●, ●, Down, Up, Down, and Right. You'll hear a sound when entered correctly. You can race as Ripper Roo in all modes except Adventure mode.

Invisibility

INVISIBILITY

At the Main Menu, press and hold L1 + R1 and press Up, Up, Down, Right, Right, and Up. You'll hear a sound when entered correctly.

99 WUMPA FRUIT/ALWAYS JUICED

At the Main Menu, press and hold L1 + R1 and press Down, Right, Right, Down, and Down. You'll hear a sound when entered correctly.

UNLIMITED MASKS

At the Main Menu, press and hold L1 + R1 and press Left, ▲, Right, Left, ●, Right, Down, and Down. You'll hear a sound when entered correctly.

Unlimited Masks

SCRAPBOOK OPTION

At the Main Menu, press and hold L1 + R1 and press Up, Up, Down, Right, Right, Left, Right, ▲, and Right. You'll hear a sound when entered correctly. In addition, a new option appears on the Main Menu called "Scrapbook."

Scrapbook Option

Turbo Counter

TURBO COUNTER

At the Main Menu, press and hold L1 + R1 and press ▲, Down, Down, ●, Up. You'll hear a sound when entered correctly.

SUPER TURBO PADS

At the Main Menu, press and hold L1 + R1 and press ▲, Right, Right, ●, and Left. You'll hear a sound when entered correctly.

SPYRO: RIPTO'S RAGE DEMO

At the Main Menu, press and hold L1 + R1 and press Down, ●, ▲, and Right.

DAVE MIRRA FREESTYLE BMX

UNLOCK SLIM JIM

At the Rider Select screen, press Down, Down, Left, Right, Up, Up, Circle.

Slim Jim — Spicy!

Unlock All Bikes

ALL BIKES

At the Bike Select screen, press Up, Left, Up, Down, Up, Right, Left, Right, Circle.

ALL STYLES

At the Style Select screen, press Left, Up, Right, Down, Left, Down, Right, Up, Left, Circle.

DIE HARD TRILOGY 2

DEBUG MENU

At the Main Menu, press L1, L1, ●, ●, ■, ■ to access a movie player and level select.

3RD PERSON ACTION/ADVENTURE MODE

INVINCIBILITY

During gameplay, pause the game and press ▲, ▲, ●, ●, L1, L2.

ALL WEAPONS

During gameplay, pause the game and press ■, ■, ●, ●, L1, L1.

INFINITE AMMO

During gameplay, pause the game and press L1, L1, R1, R1, ●, ●.

SLOW ROCKETS

During gameplay, pause the game and press L1, R1, R1, L1, ▲, ■.

DISABLE LASER SIGHTING

During gameplay, pause the game and press L1, L1, ▲, ▲, L1, L1.

HEADS POP OFF

During gameplay, pause the game and press ■, ■, ●, ●, R1, R1.

SKELETON

During gameplay, pause the game and press ●, ■, ▲, ▲, ■, ●.

GIVE ENEMIES BIG HEAD

During gameplay, pause the game and press R1, R1, L1, L1, ▲, ▲.

ELECTRIC

During gameplay, pause the game and press ■, ■, L1, L1, R1, R1.

1ST-PERSON VIEW

During gameplay, pause the game and press ●, ▲, ▲, ■.

DAMPEN CAMERA

During gameplay, pause the game and press ▲, ▲, ▲, ■, ■, ■.

EXTREME DRIVING MODE

INVINCIBILITY

During gameplay, pause the game and press ▲, ▲, ●, ●, L1, L2.

UNLIMITED TIME

During gameplay, pause the game and press L1, R1, ■, ■, R1, L1.

UNLIMITED NITRO

During gameplay, pause the game and press L1, L1, R1, R1, ●, ●.

FASTER CAR

During gameplay, pause the game and press ●, ■, R1, R1, ●, L1.

ONLY WHEELS

During gameplay, pause the game and press L1, R1, R1, L1, L1, R1.

RAIN

During gameplay, pause the game and press ■, ■, L1, L1, ▲, ●.

SHARPSHOOTER MODE

INVINCIBILITY

During gameplay, pause the game and press ▲, ▲, ●, ●, L1, L2.

UNLIMITED AMMO

During gameplay, pause the game and press L1, L1, R1, R1, ●, ●.

SLOW ROCKETS

During gameplay, pause the game and press L1, R1, R1, L1, ▲, ■.

ALL WEAPONS

During gameplay, pause the game and press ■, ■, ●, ●, L1, L1.

SLOW MOTION

During gameplay, pause the game and press ▲, L1, ▲, L1, ▲, L1.

AUTO RELOAD

During gameplay, pause the game and press ■, ■, ▲, ▲, ●, ●.

FEAR EFFECT 2: RETRO HELIX

CHEAT MODE

First you must complete the game and start a new game. Once you have control of Hana, you should come to a console. Enter the following codes:

Cheat Menu

continued

EFFECT	CODE
Big Head	10397
All Weapons	11692
Infinite Ammo	61166

Infinite Ammo

Gallery

ART GALLERIES

At the title screen, enter the following codes for the respective disc to open the Art Gallery. You can find the Art Gallery in the Extras section of the Options menu.

DISC	CODE
One	Left, Right, Up, Down, Down, ●
Two	Up, Up, R1, R1, R1, ■
Three	L1, R2, L1, R2, L1, ■
Four	●, ●, ■, L2, ■

Cool Pics!

FISHERMAN'S BAIT: A BASS CHALLENGE

TOTAL COUNT SCREEN

At the Title screen, press Up, Up, Down, Down, L1, R1, L1, R1, **x**, and ●. At the Option screen, press Select to access the Total Count.

Total Count Screen

FROGGER 2: SWAMPY'S REVENGE

All of the following codes should be entered in the in-game menu. Enter the code while holding ■. Release ■ to finish the code.

All Characters

ALL CHARACTERS

Left, Right, Left, Left, Left, Up, Left, Left

TEMPORARY INVULNERABILITY

Left, Left, Up, Left, Down, Right, Right, Right

INFINITE LIVES

Down, Down, Up, Down, Right, Down, Up, Up

Invulnerable Frog

17

LEVEL SKIP

Right, Left, Up, Up, Up, Right, Left, Left

Level Skip (1.4 sec)

Level Select

LEVEL SELECT

Up, Down, Left, Right, Right, Right, Down, Left

CHANGE COINS TO MAD GARIBS

Right, Left, Right, Left, Up, Up, Left, Right

GRIND SESSION

ALL TRICKS

In Tournament Mode, pause the game and press Down, Left, Up, Right, Down, Left, Up, Right.

All Tricks

KILLER LOOP

GET PULSE CLASS 2

At the Main Menu, press and hold Start and press Up, Left, Up, Left, Down, Left, Up, Left.

GET PULSE CLASS 3

At the Main Menu, press and hold Start and press Down, Left, Up, Left, Down, Right, Up, Right.

GET PULSE CLASS 4

At the Main Menu, press and hold Start and press Down, Left, Up, Right, Down, Right, Up, Left.

Pulse Class 4

GET H&K CLASS 2

At the Main Menu, press and hold Start and press Down, Left, Up, Left, Down, Right, Up, Left.

H&K Class 3

GET H&K CLASS 3

At the Main Menu, press and hold Start and press Down, Left, Up, Right, Down, Left, Up, Right.

GET H&K CLASS 4

At the Main Menu, press and hold Start and press Down, Right, Up, Left, Down, Left, Up, Right.

KNOCKOUT KINGS 2001

HIDDEN BOXERS

Enter the following names in the career mode to unlock these hidden boxers:

ENTER THIS NAME	TO OPEN THIS HIDDEN BOXER:
100%	Full stats

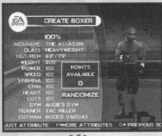

Full Stats

BABY	Baby

Baby Boxer

BULLDOG	Bulldog

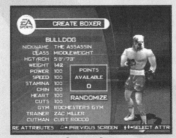

Bow-wow Boxer

CLOWN	Clown

Bozo Boxer

EYE	One Eye

Cyclops

GORE	Gorilla

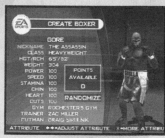

Gorilla

NOLAN	Owen Nolan
FRANCIS	Steve Francis

LEGACY OF KAIN: SOUL REAVER

REFILL HEALTH

Pause the game, press and hold L1, and then press Down, ●, Up, Left, Up, Left.

NEXT LEVEL HEALTH

Pause the game, press and hold L1, and then press Right, **X**, Left, ▲, Up, Down.

MAXIMUM HEALTH

Pause the game, press and hold L1, and then press Right, ●, Down, Up, Down, Up.

Maximum Health

REFILL MAGIC

Pause the game, press and hold L1, and then press Right, Right, Left, ▲, Right, Down.

MAXIMUM MAGIC

Pause the game, press and hold L1, and then press ▲, Right, Down, Right, Up, ▲, Left.

PASS THROUGH BARRIERS

Pause the game, press and hold L1, and then press Down, ●, ●, Left, Right, ▲, Up.

WALL CLIMBING

Pause the game, press and hold L1, and then press ▲, Down, L2, Right, Up, Down.

HURT RAZIEL

Pause the game, press and hold L1, and then press Left, ●, Up, Up, Down.

FORCE

Pause the game, press and hold L1, and then press Left, Right, ●, Left, Right, Left.

CONSTRICT

Pause the game, press and hold L1, and then press Down, Up, Right, Right, ●, Up, Up, Down.

FORCE GLYPH

Pause the game, press and hold L1, and then press Down, Left, ▲, Down, Up.

Force Glyph

STONE GLYPH

Pause the game, press and hold L1, and then press Down, ●, Up, Left, Down, Right, Right.

SOUND GLYPH

Pause the game, press and hold L1, and then press Right, Right, Down, ●, Up, Up, Down.

WATER GLYPH

Pause the game, press and hold L1, and then press Down, ●, Up, Down, Right.

SUNLIGHT GLYPH

Pause the game, press and hold L1, and then press Left, ●, Left, Right, Right, Up, Up, Left.

FIRE GLYPH

Pause the game, press and hold L1, and then press Up, Up, Right, Up, ▲, L2, Right.

SHIFT AT ANY TIME

Pause the game, press and hold L1, and then press Up, Up, Down, Right, Right, Left, ●, Right, Left, Down.

LUNAR: SILVER STAR STORY

PLAY PONG MINI GAME

After starting the game and while the FMV plays, press Up, Down, Left, Right, ▲, Start

SEE FMV SEQUENCES

After starting the game and while the FMV plays, press Up, Down, Left, Right, ▲, Start. Swap the disc with either of the other game discs to see the FMV sequences.

MARCH MADNESS 2000

HIDDEN TEAMS

Select Exhibition Mode and enter the name **EASPORTS**.

MAT HOFFMAN'S PRO BMX

HIDDEN COURSES

THPS1 WAREHOUSE

Score 200,000 with a single trick or combo to open up The Warehouse, the first level from *Tony Hawk's Pro Skater*

Warehouse

THPS1 BURNSIDE

Complete Career Mode with all eight pros (30 Covers and 2 Gold Medals each) to open up Burnside, a level from *Tony Hawk's Pro Skater*.

Burnside

SECRET CODES

At the Pause menu (during a session in a level, press start), hold L1 and enter the following codes.

8 MINUTES ADDED TO YOUR RUN TIME

■, Up, ●, X

Entering the following codes will toggle the cheat on and off.

BIG TIRES

Down, ●, ●, Down

SPECIAL BAR ALWAYS FULL

Left, Down, ▲, ●, Up, Left, ▲, ■

GRIND BALANCE BAR

Left, ●, ■, ▲, ■, ●, X

PERFECT BALANCE

■, Left, Up, Right

ALL SCORES MULTIPLIED BY 10

■, ●, ●, Up, Down, Down

ALL SCORES DIVIDED BY 10

Down, Down, Up, ●, ●, ■

TONY HAWK

Complete Career Mode with any Pro (all 30 Covers) to unlock Tony Hawk.

GRANNY

Retry a course in Career Mode 10 times without completing it to unlock Granny for your next attempt. Granny will be unlocked for good once she goes back inside for tea.

VIDEOS

Complete Career Mode with any medal in each of the two competitions to unlock the rider's highlight video.

Score two medals in Career Mode with Tony Hawk to unlock the Bails video.

Win two medals in Career Mode with Granny to unlock her secret video!

MAXED BIKES

Complete Career Mode with a Gold Medal in each of the two competitions to unlock a 4th and final bike for your rider. This bike has maximum stats so no pre-ride tinkering is ever needed!

MEDAL OF HONOR: UNDERGROUND

MOHU TEAM PICTURES

Enter **MOHUEQUIPE** as a password at the Options menu.

MOHU Pics

Cartoons!

CARTOON GALLERY

Enter **MOHDESSINS** as a password at the Options menu.

DREAMWORKS INTERACTIVE PICTURES

Enter **DWIECRANS** as a password at the Options menu.

MISSION: IMPOSSIBLE

GREETINGS PAGE

Enter **TTOPFSECRETT** as a password.

FMVS

Enter **SEECOOLMOVIE** as a password.

Greetings Page

DISABLE ANIMATION

Enter **SCAREDSTIFFF** as a password. This will give you a Bad Password message.

SLOW MOTION

Enter **IMTIREDTODAY** as a password. This will give you a Bad Password message.

SUPER JUMPS

Enter **BIONICJUMPER** as a password. This will give you a Bad Password message.

TURBO MODE

Enter **GOOUTTAMYWAY** as a password. This will give you a Bad Password message.

POSSIBLE PASSWORDS

ICE HIT

MISSION	PASSWORD
Subpen	ABEMJQLNVTPG

RECOVER NOC LIST

MISSION	PASSWORD
Embassy Function	OGLIESHVIRLL
Warehouse	OQRFFSITJMNI
KGB HQ	EHNJHSURWJMP
Security Hallway	GDPSISJOWUAN
Sewage Control	GGHIHSJVWRML
Escape (Security Hallway)	GQOFISKTLMAI
Escape (KGB HQ)	IGCJMJMVMRBL
Fire Alarm	IQDSNJNTOMCI

CIA ESCAPE

MISSION	PASSWORD
Interrogation	IJENMUNHONCJ
Interrogation (Hallway)	IMQPNHNKOSCM
Interrogation (Infirmary)	PBFROUOPPWDB
CIA Rooftop	PMGKPUPKQSDM
Terminal Room	PJGNOUPHQNDJ
Rooftop Escape	KEJPPUPSRKEE

MOLE HUNT

MISSION	PASSWORD
Station	HDGGFPKQMOBC
Train Car	IGILGPMLMYBO
Train Car	HDGOFTKQMOBC
Train Roof	IGJDGTMLMYBO

ICE STORM

MISSION	PASSWORD
Subpen	NGHSMGQTXMGI
Tunnel	MOEEOJGHVXJH
Mainland	MKEHTJSSVVJD
Gunboat	AFQMOJGPVTPG

IMPOSSIBLE PASSWORDS

Impossible Passwords

ICE HIT

MISSION	PASSWORD
Subpen	HILKJTKUMLBF

RECOVER NOC LIST

MISSION	PASSWORD
Embassy Function	PMCQEQPJQQDQ
Warehouse	KNDPFTPLQYDO
KGB HQ	LDEESUVPRWGB
Security Hallway	LFERHGVRXJGP
Sewage Control	LBEHSFVNRTGG
Escape(Security Hallway)	LPEKSMVQXOGC
Escape(KGB HQ)	NIQNKRQUSLHF
Fire Alarm	NQQQKLRHSNHJ

CIA ESCAPE

MISSION	PASSWORD
Interrogation	AMRQMQSJNQPQ
Interrogation (Hallway)	BBMENISNNTKG
Interrogation (Infirmary)	CENHOQGWIVLD
CIA Rooftop	CINKPTGUILLF
Terminal Room	BQMMTUGHUNKJ
Rooftop Escape	BOMNOGGVURKL

MOLE HUNT

MISSION	PASSWORD
Station	MEPHFQTWVVJD
Train Car	MIPKGTTUVLJF
Train Car	FLNNEPTITPIK
Train Roof	MGNQFHTKTSIM

ICE STORM

MISSION	PASSWORD
Subpen	DHIJLSIRKJFP
Tunnel	DKILMIUMKXFH
Mainland	OMGSKPIIJPNK
Gunboat	DNGOLHIKJSNM

NASCAR 2001

CODES

Enter the Credits menu located in the Options menu and then select Development. Make sure to enter the codes after the movie and during the credits to access the following extras.

ENTER THIS CODE	TO ACCESS...
Hold L2 and press: ■, ●, ▲, ✕	Asher Boldt

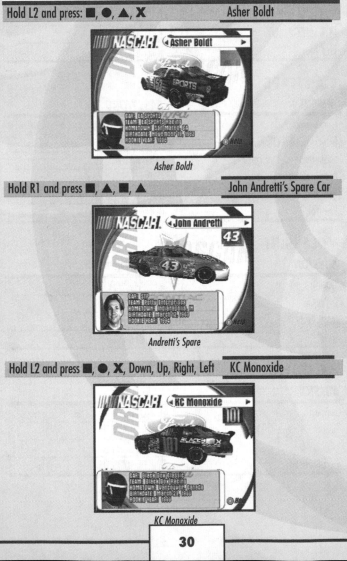

Asher Boldt

Hold R1 and press ■, ▲, ■, ▲	John Andretti's Spare Car

Andretti's Spare

Hold L2 and press ■, ●, ✕, Down, Up, Right, Left	KC Monoxide

KC Monoxide

Hold R2 and press ■, ●, ✗, Up, Down, Left, Right   Shorty Leung

Shorty Leung

Hold L1 and press ■, ▲, ■, ●, ■, ✗   Jocko Micaels

Jocko Micaels

Hold R1 and press Left, ●, Up, Down, Right, Right, Right   Proving Grounds Track

Proving Grounds

continued

ENTER THIS CODE	TO ACCESS...
Hold L2 and press ■, ●, ■, Up, Up, Down, Up, Left, Right, **X**	Treasure Island Track

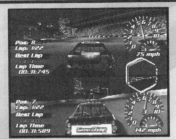

Treasure Island

NASCAR RUMBLE

ALL CARS AND COURSES

Enter **C9P5AU8NAA** as a password at the Load and Save Game Option.

All Cars and Courses

NBA HOOPZ

CHEAT CODES

After selecting your team(s), use the ■, **X**, and ● to input the following codes—each button press should change an icon on the versus screen. The first number is the number of times you press ■, the second is for **X** and the third is for ●. After entering the correct number of button presses, press the joystick or d-pad in the noted direction.

For example, for Infinite Turbo you would press ■ three times, **X** once and ● twice. Then press Up. The words Infinite Turbo will appear above the icons.

EFFECT	CODE
No Fouls (Teams must agree)	2-2-2 Right
No goaltending	4-4-4 Left

EFFECT	CODE
No Hotspots (Teams must agree)	3-0-1 Up
Show Hotspot	1-1-0 Down
Infinite Turbo	3-1-2 Up
Granny Shots	1-2-1 Left
Show Shot %	0-1-1 Down
Home Uniform	0-1-4 Right
Away Uniform	0-2-4 Right
ABA Ball	1-1-1 Right
Big Heads	3-0-0 Right
Tiny heads	3-3-0 Left
Tiny players	5-4-3 Left
Beach court	0-2-3 Left
Street court	3-2-0 Left

NEED FOR SPEED V-RALLY 2

ALL CARS, TROPHIES, AND LEVELS

Select Game Progress from the Options Menu, and press L1, R1, Left, Right, Left, Right, Up, Down, Up, Down, **X**, **X** ı Soloct.

NFL XTREME 2

Select the Rosters/Create Player option, and enter the following as a the first and last name:

CODE	ENTER
Large Players	BIG BEN

Large Players

continued

CODE	ENTER
Small Players	TINY TOM

Small Players

Big Heads	BIGHEAD BOBBY
Flat Heads	COINHEAD COREY
Long Necks	GEORGE GIRAFFE
Long Arms	MONKEY MICKEY
Short Arms	SHRIMPY SEAN
Reversed Animations	LAMEBOY LENNY
Urban Field	CITY SCAPE

Urban Field

Lunar Field	LUNAR FIELD
Aircraft Carrier Field	AIRCRAFT CARRIER

Aircraft Carrier Field

| Egyptian Field | EGYPT SPHINX |
| Pool Table Field | POOL TABLE |

Pool Table Field

NIGHTMARE CREATURES 2

LEVEL SELECT

At the Main Menu, press and hold R2 + L1 + ● + ■ and press Select. After doing so, text appears in the top-left corner of the screen enabling you to choose a level.

GAME CHEATS

During gameplay, pause the game and press and hold R2 + L1 + ● + ■ and press Select. A new menu called Hero Unlimited Lives appears. With this code, you won't take damage from enemy attacks.

After accessing this menu, use the following key commands to access these additional cheats.

UNLIMITED ENEMY LIVE

■ + ● + Select

UNLIMITED POWER UP

L1 + R1 + Select

Display Hero Live

L2 + R2 + ■ + Select

Unlimited Continue

L1 + R2 + R1 + Select

Kill Enemy

L1 + L2 + R1 + ■ + Select

PAC MAN WORLD

INVINCIBILITY
Pause the game and press Up, Down, Right, L2, L2, L2, Right, Left, Up.

PONG

FIRST LEVEL
At the Zone Select screen, pause the game and press L1, R1, L1, R1.

SECOND LEVEL
At the Zone Select screen, pause the game and press L2, R2, L2, R2.

THIRD LEVEL, POWER-UPS, AND CLASSIC PONG
At the Zone Select screen, pause the game and press L1 + R1 + L2 + R2.

LEVEL SELECT
At the Options screen, press L1, R1, L1, R1, L1, R1.

POWER SPIKE PRO BEACH VOLLEYBALL

ALL COURTS

While Option is highlighted, press ■, ▲, ●, ▲, ■. A tone will sound if you have entered the code correctly.

All Courts

QUAKE II

INVINCIBILITY

Pause the game and press L2, L2, R1, R2, R1, L2.

RAZOR FREESTYLE SCOOTER

UNLOCK TRACKS, RIDERS AND SCOOTERS

Pause the game and press Right, Down, Right, Left, Right, Up, Right, Right. You will hear a sound if entered correctly.

RC STUNT COPTER

UNLOCK LEVELS

At the Main Menu press Down, Up, Right, Left, ▲, X, ■, ●. You will hear "Cheaters Never Prosper" when entered correctly.

ALL GOLD

At the Main Menu press Down, Up, Left, Right, ▲, X, ■, ●. You will hear "Cheaters Never Prosper" when entered correctly.

All Gold

MEGA POINTS

At the Main Menu press L2, R2, L1, R1, ▲, ●, X, ■. You will hear "Cheaters Never Prosper" when entered correctly.

LONGER NAME

At the Main Menu press Up, Down, Left, Right, ▲, X, ■, ●. You will hear "Cheaters Never Prosper" when entered correctly.

Longer Name

RESIDENT EVIL 3: NEMESIS

SECRET COSTUMES

After the credits, you'll see a screen showing the Boutique Key. This item unlocks the door to the Boutique in Uptown, which is shown in the background. There are new costumes inside for Jill.

Secret Costumes

You will also have a number of new outfits for Jill to try on in the Boutique. If you get an "E" rank, you get one additional costume, a "D" rank gets two, up until you have all five. So, if you get a "D" rank and then a "C" rank, you'll have all five costumes.

Alternate Costumes

THE MERCENARIES: OPERATION MAD JACKAL BONUS GAME

After defeating the game, you can reload your save game to play the bonus game.

RE-VOLT

ALL CARS
Enter **CARNIVAL** as a name.

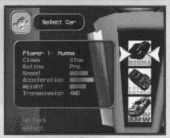

All Cars

All Tracks

ALL TRACKS
Enter **TRACKER** as a name.

ROLLCAGE STAGE 2

ALL TRACKS, CARS, MODES, AND MORE
Enter **I.WANT.IT.ALL.AND.I.WANT.IT.NOW!** as your password.

ATD GHOST CARS
Enter **WLL.IF.IT.AINT.THEM.PESKY.KIDS** as your password.

DEMOLITION MODES
Enter **IS.IT.COLD.IN.HERE.OR.IS.IT.JUST.ME?** as your password.

MEGA SPEED
Enter **LOOK.OUT!.ITS.ANDY.GREEN** as your password.

MIRROR MODE
Enter **I.AM.THE.MIRROR.MAN,.OOOOOOOOOO!** as your password.

PURSUIT MODE
Enter **PURSUIT,.A.SUIT.MADE.FROM.CATS** as your password.

RUBBLE SOCCER MODE

Enter **IM.OBVIOUSLY.SICK.AS.A.PARROT** as your password.

SURVIVOR MODE

Enter **HERE.TODAY,.GONE,.LATE.AFTERNOON** as your password.

ALL COMBAT TRACKS

Enter **YOU.HAVE.A.LOTA.EXPLODING.TO.DO** as your password.

ALL TRACKS

Enter **NOW.THAT'S.WHAT.I.CALL.RACING.147** as your password.

ALL CARS

Enter **WHEELS,.METAL,.ITS.....THE.BIN!** as your password.

MORE DIFFICULT MASTERS

Enter **MASTERS.IS.AS.HARD.AS.NAILS.MON!** as your password.

RUSHDOWN

ALL TRACKS (ARCADE MODE)

At the Main Menu, press Up, Up, Down, Down, Left, Right, Left, Right, ▲, ●, ▲, ●.

All Tracks (Arcade Mode)

SAMMY SOSA HIGH HEAT BASEBALL 2001

DIFFERENT CLOUDS

While in the Stadium Select screen, enter the following codes for some different cloud effects:

3DO Clouds: L2, R2, L2, R2, ■, ■

Wacky Clouds: R2, L2, ■, L1, R1, ■

SIMPSONS WRESTLING

NEW CHALLENGER CIRCUIT
DEFENDER CIRCUIT
CHAMPION CIRCUIT
CONTINUE TOURNAMENT
PRACTICE GAME
VS MATCH GAME
OPTIONS
BONUS MATCH UP
PRESS ⊗ TO SELECT AN ITEM

Bonus Match

BONUS MATCH UP

At the title screen press ●, Up, Up, Down, Down, Left, Right, Left, Right.

WRESTLE AS BUMBLE BEE MAN

Defeat Bumble Bee Man in the New Challenger Circuit.

WRESTLE AS FRINK

Defeat Frink in the Champion Circuit.

WRESTLE AS MOE THE BARTENDER

Defeat Moe in the Defender Circuit.

WRESTLE AS NED FLANDERS

Defeat Ned Flanders in the Champion Circuit.

SNO-CROSS CHAMPIONSHIP RACING

These codes should be entered while at the main menu. Hold the R1 button, enter the code and then release the R1 button to finish the code.

RACE ON AN ATV

Up, Right, Down, Up, Right, Down

ATV

GoCart Mayhem

RACE ON A GOCART

Right, Right, Left, Left, Right, Right

UNLOCK SECRET CARTOON TRACK

Right, Up, Left, ●, ▲, ■

Choose the single-player mode and race on the Kiruna Track to see the cartoon landscape.

Cartoon Track

Summer Track

UNLOCK THE SUMMER TRACK

▲, X, ●, ●, X, ▲

UNLOCK EVERY LEAGUE, SNOWMOBILE AND TRACK

Up, ▲, Up, ▲, Up, ▲

LAUNCH THE DEMO MODE

Up, Up, Up, Down, Down, Down

SOUTH PARK

Enter the following cheats at the Cheat Menu:

CODE	ENTER
Master Cheat	ZBOBBYBIRD

Master Cheat.

Chef in Multiplayer	YLOVEMACHINE
Wendy in Multiplayer	BCHECKATACO
Terrence in Multiplayer	SRAFT
Phillip in Multiplayer	PPHAERT
Ned in Multiplayer	JHAWKING
Mr. Mackey in Multiplayer	ACHEATINGSBAD
Officer Barbrady in Multiplayer	DELVISLIVES
Big Gay Al in Multiplayer	GOUTRANGE
Starvin' Marvin in Multiplayer	MSLAPUPMEAL
Mr. Garrison in Multiplayer	VDOROTHYSFRIEND
Pip in Multiplayer	EFISHNCHIPS
Jimbo in Multiplayer	QSTARINGFROG
Ike in Multiplayer	HKICKME
Ms. Cartman in Multiplayer	KALLWOMAN
Mephisto in Multiplayer	NGOODSCIENCE
Alien Visitor in Multiplayer	TMAJESTIC

SPEC OPS: STEALTH PATROL

INVULNERABILITY

When prompted to enter your name, enter the word ROCKSTAR. Pause the game and you will have the ability to toggle the option on or off.

Invulnerability

SPIDER-MAN

BIG HEAD

Select Special/Cheats and enter DULUX.

INVINCIBLE

Select Special/Cheats and enter RUSTCRST.

LEVEL SELECT

Select Special/Cheats and enter XCLSIOR. This will open a new option in the Cheats menu.

UNLIMITED WEBBING

Select Special/Cheats and enter STRUDL.

UNLOCK COMIC BOOK COVERS IN GALLERY

Select Special/Cheats and enter ALLSIXCC.

UNLOCK MOVIES IN GALLERY

Select Special/Cheats and enter WATCH EM.

UNLOCK J JAMES JEWETT IN GALLERY

Select Special/Cheats and enter RULUR.

UNLOCK EVERYTHING

Select Special/Cheats and enter EEL NATS.

SPORTS CAR GT

MORE MONEY

At the Title screen, press Up, Left, Left, Right, Down, Right, L1, ■.

More Money

ALL CLASSES AND TRACKS

At the Title screen, press Down, Down, Left, Right, Up, Left, ●, R2.

SPYRO 2: RIPTO'S RAGE!

FIND GEMS

Press and hold L1 + L2 + R1 + R2 and Sparks will point to the nearest gem.

GET ALL ABILITIES

Pause the game and press ● (X4) and ■.

BIG HEAD MODE

Pause the game and press Up (X4), R1 (X4), ●.

Big Head Mode

Flat Spyro

FLAT SPYRO

Pause the game and press Left, Right, Left, Right, L2, R2, L2, R2, ■.

BLUE SPYRO

Pause the game and press Up, Right, Down, Left, Up, ■, R1, R2, L1, L2, Up, Left, Down, Right, Up, **X**.

GREEN SPYRO

Pause the game and press Up, Right, Down, Left, Up, ■, R1, R2, L1, L2, Up, Left, Down, Right, Up, ▲.

PINK SPYRO

Pause the game and press Up, Right, Down, Left, Up, ■, R1, R2, L1, L2, Up, Left, Down, Right, Up, ■.

RED SPYRO

Pause the game and press Up, Right, Down, Left, Up, ■, R1, R2, L1, L2, Up, Left, Down, Right, Up, ●.

YELLOW SPYRO

Pause the game and press Up, Right, Down, Left, Up, ■, R1, R2, L1, L2, Up, Left, Down, Right, Up, Up.

BLACK SPYRO

Pause the game and press Up, Right, Down, Left, Up, ■, R1, R2, L1, L2, Up, Left, Down, Right, Up, Down.

VIEW ENDING CREDITS

Pause the game and press ■, ●, ■, ●, ■, ●, Left, Right, Left, Right, Left, Right.

CRASH TEAM RACING PLAYABLE DEMO

At the Title screen, press and hold L1 + R2 and press ■.

SPYRO: YEAR OF THE DRAGON

Pause your game and enter the following codes to get the desired effect.

2D SPYRO

Left, Right, Left, Right, L1, R1, L1, R1, ■, ●

Enter the code again to change Spyro back to full 3D.

2 Dimensional

BIG HEAD

Up, R1, Up, R1, Up, R1, ●, ●, ●, ●

Enter the code again to change Spyro's head back to normal.

Big Head

Black Spyro

BLACK SPYRO

Up, Left, Down, Right, Up, ■, R1, R2, L1, L2, Up, Right, Down, Left, Up, Down

BLUE SPYRO

Up, Left, Down, Right, Up, ■, R1, R2, L1, L2, Up, Right, Down, Left, Up, **X**

GREEN SPYRO

Up, Left, Down, Right, Up, ■, R1, R2, L1, L2, Up, Right, Down, Left, Up, ▲

PINK SPYRO

Up, Left, Down, Right, Up, ■, R1, R2, L1, L2, Up, Right, Down, Left, Up, ■

RED SPYRO

Up, Left, Down, Right, Up, ■, R1, R2, L1, L2, Up, Right, Down, Left, Up, ●

YELLOW SPYRO

Up, Left, Down, Right, Up, ■, R1, R2, L1, L2, Up, Right, Down, Left, Up, Up

ORIGINAL COLOR SPYRO

To change Spyro back to his original color enter Up, Left, Down, Right, Up, ■, R1, R2, L1, L2, Up, Right, Down, Left, Up, Left.

Roll Credits

CREDITS

Left, Right, Left, Right, Left, Right, ■, ●, ■, ●, ■, ●

CRASH BASH DEMO

You'll have to enter this code at the Title Screen. Once there, press L1 + R2 + ■.

STAR WARS EPISODE 1: JEDI POWER BATTLES

PLAY AS DARTH MAUL

Defeat the game with Qui-Gon Jinn.

SUPERCROSS 2001

CHEAT CODES

Select Options/Cheat Codes and enter the following:

CODE	EFFECT
UNLIMITEDPC	Unlimited power clutch
JOKERIDERS	All joke riders
NOBIKES	Invisible bikes
NORIDERS	Invisible riders
NDFSPD	Unlimited turbo
LOFENCES	Low fences
I AM WEAK	Display riders weakness
EXPLODE	Exploding text
OTRATTWTGHWG	The Riverbed Track
OSSFMOGLFM	The Launching Pad Track
WMXPLIBWWA	The Washougal Track
NUTSANDBOLTSS	Parts Unlimited Championship
NEEDNEWEXHAUST	FMF Championship
SUPPLIESONLINE	Wrenchead.com Championship
SHOESANDTRICKS	Etnies Freestyle Games
THROWMEGOGGLES	Scott Championship

HIDDEN RIDERS

Select Options/Cheat Codes and enter the following:

CODE	CHARACTER
4XUSMXDNCHAMP	Johnny O'Marra
9XBELGIANCHAMP	Roger DeCoster
BUNGAVEE	Space Overlord
DTMHBOSS	Bradley G
ENDZONEDANCE	Smitty Sugarlegs
FORTYFOUR	Bob Page
HARVEYSAYSRELAX	Hot Tub Harvey
HONORFIRST	Moto Samurai
IRONMAN	David Bailey
JOUSTER	Sir Dirthead
LETSGOEAGAL	EA Gal
LOVESBRAINS	The Zombie
LOOKMANOBODY	Doctor Invizzo
MARROWMAN	Bones
MASKEDMAN	El Luchador
MELLOWOUT	Tie Dye Guy
METALDUDE	MR-34 Robot
MMMSQUIRREL	Harry Bigfoot
ONESMALLSTEP	Astro Nut
PEANUTBUTTER	Agent Albert
PLAIDROCKS	Brave Scotsman
POSSUMPANCAKES	Billy Ray MudMullet
POLKADOT	Tricky The Clown
PYRAMIDSCHEME	Sarcophagus Jones
SIDEBURNS	The King
SQWAK	Marimba
THREEPIECESUIT	Spitt Polish
TRIPLELEAPER	Supercross Avenger
WHOSTHAT	Some Guy
WWWECKOCOM	Ecko Rider

TEST DRIVE OFF-ROAD 3

Master Code

MASTER CODE

Enter **ZAKARY X** as a name. You can then turn on the cheats at the Cheat Menu in the Options screen.

STUNT MODE (TURN IN MID-AIR)

Enter **TURN TRICKS** as a name.

SUMO-STYLE (INCREASE COLLISION EFFECTS)

Enter **YOKOZUNA** as a name.

ALL DIVISIONS

Enter **SAD CLOWN** as a name.

ALL TRACKS

Enter **LEAD TO ROME** as a name.

All Divisions

All Upgrades

ALL UPGRADES

Enter **MAD HOOKUP** as a name.

THE MUMMY

CHEATS

Start a game, then pause and quit. Select Replay Level and then Bonus Features.
Enter the following:

EFFECT	CHEAT
Cairo Bonus Level	▲, X, ▲, ●, ■, ▲, ●, X
Invincibility	▲, X, ●, ●, X, ■, ■, X
Infinite Lives	●, ●, ▲, ●, X, ■, ■, X
Infinite Ammo	X, ▲, X, ■, ●, ▲, ■, ▲
All Weapons	●, ■, ●, X, X, ▲, ▲, ■

THRASHER: SKATE AND DESTROY

EXTRA POINTS

During a timed run, pause the game. Then press and hold L1 + R2 and repeatedly
press ● to increase your score 5,000 points at a time.

Bumblebee Suit

BUMBLEBEE SUIT

Select Roach without a hat and enter
beesuitguy as a name.

TOMB RAIDER CHRONICLES

UNLOCK UNLIMITED HEALTH, AMMO AND WEAPONS

While in the game, press Select to access your inventory screen. Highlight the Timex and enter the following secret code:

Hold Up + R1 + L1 + L2 + R2 then press ▲.

Limitless

Unlock Items

UNLOCK EVERY ITEM FOR YOUR LEVEL

While in the game, press Select to access your inventory screen. Highlight the Timex and enter the following secret code:

Hold Down + R1 + L1 + L2 + R2 then press ▲.

This will also give you the Special Features option at the main menu.

Special Features

START AT SECOND ADVENTURE

Highlight the New Game option at the main menu and enter the following secret code:

Hold L1 + Up then press **X** to start at the Russian Base.

START AT THIRD ADVENTURE

Highlight the New Game option at the main menu and enter the following secret code:

Hold L2 + Up then press **X** to start at the Black Isle.

START AT FOURTH ADVENTURE

Highlight the New Game option at the main menu and enter the following secret code:

Hold R1 + Up then press **X** to start at the Tower Block.

TOMB RAIDER: THE LAST REVELATION

TIP: An easy way to face North in the game is to find a ledge facing South and jump up and hang on it.

ALL SECRET ITEMS

Face north, highlight the Large Medipack in your inventory, hold L1 + L2 + R1 + R2 + Down, and press ▲ when the needle faces directly north.

All Secret Items

Unlimited Items

UNLIMITED ITEMS

Face north, highlight the Small Medipack in your inventory, hold L1 + L2 + R1 + R2, and press Up when the needle faces directly north.

ALL WEAPONS AND UNLIMITED AMMO

Face north, highlight the Small Medipack in your inventory, hold L1 + L2 + R1 + R2 + Up, and press ▲ when the needle faces directly north.

LEVEL SKIP

Face north, highlight Load, hold L1 + L2 + R2 + R1 + Up, and press ▲ when the needle faces directly north.

Level Skip

TONY HAWK'S PRO SKATER 2

NEVERSOFT CHARACTERS

At the Main Menu, hold L1 and press Up, ■, ■, ▲, Right, Up, ●, ▲. This causes the wheel to spin. Then create a skater and give him the name of anyone on the Neversoft team. For example, name your skater Mick West and he'll appear. The best one is Connor Jewett, the son of Neversoft's President. (Don't change the appearance of the kid-sized skaters. It could crash your game.)

You must enter the following codes after pausing the game. While the game is paused, press and hold L1, and enter the codes.

JET PACK MODE

Up, Up, Up, Up, **X**, ■, Up, Up, Up, Up, **X**, ■, Up, Up, Up, Up

Hold Triangle to hover

Press X to turn on the Jetpack

Press forward to move forward

FATTER SKATER

X (x4), Left, **X** (x4), Left, **X** (x4), Left

Fatter Skater

THINNER SKATER

X (x4), ■, **X** (x4), ■, **X** (x4), ■

TOGGLE BLOOD ON/OFF
Right, Up, ■, ▲

SPECIAL METER ALWAYS YELLOW
X, ▲, ●, ●, Up, Left, ▲, ■

Special Meter On

SUPER SPEED MODE
Down, ■, ▲, Right, Up, ●, Down, ■, ▲, Right, Up, ●

UNLOCK EVERYTHING
X, X, X, ■, ▲, Up, Down, Left, Up, ■, ▲, X, ▲, ●, X, ▲, ●

Big Head

BIG HEAD
■, ●, Up, Left, Left, ■, Right, Up, Left

ALL GAPS
Down, Up, Left, Left, ●, Left, Up, ▲, ▲, Up, Right, ■, ■, Up, X

This will also give you Private Carrera.

ALL SECRET CHARACTERS
■, ●, Right, ▲, ●, Right, ●, ▲, Right, ■, Right, Up, Up, Left, Up, ■

MOON PHYSICS
X, ■, Left, Up, Down, Up, ■, ▲

DOUBLE MOON PHYSICS
Left, Up, Left, Up, Down, Up, ■, ▲, Left, Up, Left, Up, Down, Up, ■, ▲

$5000
X, Down, Left, Right, Down, Left, Right

100,000 POINTS IN COMPETITION
■, ●, Right, ■, ●, Right, ■, ●, Right

This will end the competition.

ACCESS ALL LEVELS
Up, ▲, Right, Up, ■, ▲, Right, Up, Left, ■, ■, Up, ●, ●, Up, Right

STATS AT 5
Up, ■, ▲, Up, Down

STATS AT 6
Down, ■, ▲, Up, Down

STATS AT 7
Left, ■, ▲, Up, Down

STATS AT 8
Right, ■, ▲, Up, Down

STATS AT 9
Circle, ■, ▲, Up, Down

STATS AT 13
X, ▲, ●, X, X, X, ■, ▲, Up, Down

STATS AT ALL 10'S
X, ▲, ●, ■, ▲, Up, Down

SKIP TO RESTART
■, ▲, Right, Up, Down, Up, Left, ■, ▲, Right, Up, Down, Up, Left, ●, Up, Left, ▲

CLEAR GAME WITH CURRENT SKATER
●, Left, Up, Right, ●, Left, Up, Right, X, ●, Left, Up, Right, ●, Left, Up, Right

KID MODE

●, Up, Up, Left, Left, ●, Up, Down, ■

MIRROR LEVEL

Up, Down, Left, Right, ▲, X, ■, ●, Up, Down, Left, Right, ▲, X, ■, ●

PERFECT BALANCE

Right, Up, Left, ■, Right, Up, ■, ▲

SLO-NIC MODE

●, Up, ▲, ■, X, ▲, ●

WIREFRAME

Down, ●, Right, Up, ■, ▲

SIM MODE

●, Right, Up, Left, ▲, ●, Right, Up, Down

SMOOTH SHADING

Down, Down, Up, ■, ▲, Up, Right

DISCO LIGHTS

Down, Up, ■, ●, Up, Left, Up, X

80'S TONY

Complete 100% of the game with Tony Hawk.

SPIDER-MAN

Complete 100% of the game with a custom skater.

CHEAT MENU

Complete 100% of the game with the rest of the skaters to open the following in order:

CHEAT	DESCRIPTION
Officer Dick	The first hidden character
Skip to restart	Pause the game and you can choose between starting points

continued

CHEAT	DESCRIPTION
Kid Mode	Increased stats, harder to bail tricks, kid-sized skaters
Perfect Balance	Never lose balance on grinds and manuals
Always Special	Special meter always full
STUD Cheat	Stats maxed out; It won't show in the Buy Stats screen, but it's there
Weight Cheat	Change weight of skater
Wireframe	Wireframe mode
Slow-Nic	Tricks in slow motion
Big Head Cheat	Big heads
Sim Mode	More realistic play
Smooth Cheat	No textures
Moon Physics	Bigger jumps
Disco Mode	Blinking lights
Level Flip	Levels are mirrored

PRIVATE CARRERA

Perform every gap in the game, except for Chopper Drop and Skater Heaven.

80'S TONY VIDEO

Earn three gold medals with McSqueeb (80's Tony). To view this video, start any competition, then End Run.

NEVERSOFT BAILS VIDEO

Earn three gold medals with Officer Dick.

SPIDER-MAN VIDEO

Earn three gold medals with Spider-Man

NEVERSOFT MAKES VIDEO

Earn three gold medals with Private Carrera

CHOPPER DROP: HAWAII LEVEL

Earn three gold medals with every skater.

SKATER HEAVEN

Complete 100% of the game with every skater, including secret characters.

GYMNASIUM IN SCHOOL LEVEL

Grind the Roll Call! Opunsezmee Rail with 1:40 on the clock to open the door to the gym.

TWISTED METAL 4

Enter the following codes as passwords. You will hear a sound when entered correctly.

CODE	ENTER
Play as Sweet Tooth	Start, R1, Right, Right, Left

Sweet Tooth

Play as Crusher	Down, R1, Right, R1, L1
Play as Moon Buggy	Start, ▲, Right, L1, Start
Play as RC Car	Up, Down, Left, Start, Right
Play as Super Axel	Up, Right, Down, Up, L1
Play as Minion	▲, L1, L1, Left, Up
Play as Super Auger	Left, ●, ▲, Right, Down
Play as Super Thumper	●, ▲, Start, ●, Left
Play as Super Slamm	Right, L1, Start, ●, Start

continued

Super Slamm

Powerful Special Weapons	Up, Start, ●, R1, Left
Very little traction	Down, ▲, Down, L1, R1
CPU targets humans	Right, ▲, Right, ▲, L1
All power-ups are Homing Missiles	R1, Right, Left, R1, Up
All power-ups are Napalms	Right, Left, R1, Right, ●
All power-ups are Power Missiles	Down, Down, ●, L1, Left
All power-ups are Remote Bombs	Up, Right, Down, L1, ▲
CPU ignores health	L1, Left, Right, ●, Right
Extra fast weapons	R1, L1, Down, Start, Down
Faster health regeneration	▲, L1, Down, ▲ Up
God Mode	Down, Left, L1, Left, Right
No health in deathmatch	▲, Down, ▲, ●, ▲
No health in tournament & deathmatch	Down, R1, Down, Start, ●
No power-ups	●, Start, Left, L1, Start

VIGILANTE 8: SECOND OFFENSE

Select Game Status at the Options Menu and highlight a character. Press R1 + L1 to enter the following passwords:

Status Screen

ENTER	CODE
GO_MONSTER	All Cars Big Wheels
NO_GRAVITY	Reduced Gravity
HOME_ALONE	No Enemies on Level
LONG_MOVIE	View Movies

View Movies

MIXES_CARS	Choose Same Cars (Multiplayer mode)
DRIVE_ONLY	Wheel Attachment Icons Won't Respawn
BLAST_FIRE	Extremely Deadly Missiles
RAPID_FIRE	No Weapon Fire Delay
UNDER_FIRE	Multiple Enemies Attack
GO_SLOW_MO	Slow Motion

GO_RAMMING	Heavy Cars
MORE_SPEED	Faster Cars
QUICK_PLAY	Faster Action
JACK_IT_UP	Cars on Stilts

Cars on Stilts

ORIGINAL VIGILANTE 8 LEVELS

You can access the old Vigilante 8 levels by taking out the Second Offense CD (during run-time only), and then inserting an original Vigilante 8 CD. Then wait for the message "V8 Levels Enabled," and re-insert the Second Offense CD and quit. You'll then have access to the old levels at the Level Select screen.

WU-TANG: SHAOLIN STYLE

ALL CHARACTERS

At the Main Menu, press Right (X4), Left (X4), ■, ●, ■, ●.

FIGHT AS OTIS

In VS Mode, highlight Ghostface Killer at the Character Select screen, hold the Select button, and press **X**.

All Characters.

Fight as Hystrix.

FIGHT AS HYSTRIX

In VS Mode, highlight Method Man at the Character Select screen, hold the Select button, and press **X**.

FIGHT AS GASCHE

In VS Mode, highlight Masta Killa at the Character Select screen, hold the Select button, and press **X**.

FIGHT AS XIN

In VS Mode, highlight Inspectah Deck at the Character Select screen, hold the Select button, and press **X**.

FIGHT AS LECHER

In VS Mode, highlight Ol' Dirty Bastard at the Character Select screen, hold the Select button, and press **X**.

FIGHT AS FEARMENTOR

In VS Mode, highlight RZA at the Character Select screen, hold the Select button, and press **X**.

Fearmentor

FIGHT AS SINENSIS

In VS Mode, highlight U God at the Character Select screen, hold the Select button, and press **X**.

FIGHT AS CERITH

In VS Mode, highlight GZA at the Character Select screen, hold the Select button, and press **x**.

FIGHT AS BONE GEAR

In VS Mode, highlight Raekwon at the Character Select screen, hold the Select button, and press **X**.

Bone Gear

PARENTAL LOCK PASSWORD

Enter ▲, ●, X, X, ■, ▲, ●, ■ as a password.

X-MEN: MUTANT ACADEMY

UNLOCK EVERYTHING

At the Main Menu press Select, Up, L2, R1, L1, R2. You should hear a sound if entered correctly. Press Select + Start to lock everything back.

THE GAMES

PLAYSTATION® 2

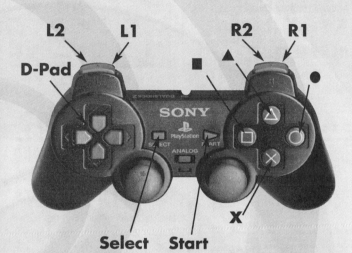

L2   L1   R2   R1

D-Pad

■   ▲   ●

X

Select   Start

4 X 4 EVOLUTION

SLOW MOTION

At the Main Menu enter L1, L2, R1, R2, ■, ●.

WARP SPEED

At the Main Menu enter L1, L2, R1, R2, ■, ■.

NORMAL SPEED

At the Main Menu enter L1, L2, R1, R2, ●, ●.

Warp Speed

ALL STAR BASEBALL 2002

Dingers & Islanders

THE AUSTIN DINGERS AND THE GLEN COVE ISLANDERS BONUS TEAMS

Select Exhibition Mode and press R2 + L2 at the team select. You should hear a sound when done correctly.

THE AUSTIN DINGERS IN BATTING PRACTICE

Select Batting Practice and press R2 + R1 + L2 + L1 at the player select. The Dingers' line-up will appear if done correctly.

Dingers Batting

ARMORED CORE 2

PLUS CHEATS

Intentionally lose the first mission after the Raven test, then die with -50,000 credits or less to activate the "Plus" cheats. The game will restart from the first level with all items gained in the previous game. Your pilot name will vanish from the "Pilot name" slot. The more times this is done, the more cheats you will unlock. Some examples are better radar (grid system that detects incoming missiles), fire projectiles from laser swords (press ●, then quickly press **X**), cooling twice as fast, being able to fire rear weapons while in motion, and double available energy.

ARMY MEN: AIR ATTACK 2

PASSWORDS

MISSION	PASSWORD
2	Up, **X**, ▲, Right, Left, ■, ●, **X**
3	▲, ●, Down, Left, ■, ■, Up, Up
4	**X**, Right, Left, **X**, ●, ■, ■, ▲
5	Down, Down, ●, ■, ●, ■, Right, **X**
6	▲, **X**, Up, Left, Right, Left, ●, ▲
7	Left, ■, Right, Down, ●, **X**, **X**, Right
8	▲, Right, ■, ■, ●, Down, Down, **X**
9	Up, **X**, ■, Left, Right, ●, Left, Left
10	▲, Up, ●, **X**, ■, Down, Down, Down
11	●, ●, Up, Left, Right, **X**, ▲, ■
13	Left, Left, ▲, ●, **X**, **X**, Down, Right
15	Left, Right, ●, **X**, ■, Down, Down, ●
16	▲, ●, **X**, Right, Right, ●, ■, Down
18	●, **X**, Right, ▲, ■, Up, **X**, **X**
20	Up, **X**, ●, Up, Left, ■, ●, **X**

Final Mission

ARMY MEN: SARGE'S HEROES 2

Enter the following codes as a password:

MODE	PASSWORD
All Levels	FREEPLAY

All Levels

All Weapons	GIMME
Immortal	NODIE
Invisible	NOSEEUM

Can't see me

Mini Mode	SHORTY
Super Sized	IMHUGE

Super Size

Test Info	THDOTEST

Test Info

PASSWORDS

MISSION	PASSWORD
Training: Boot Camp	BOOTCAMP
Mission 1: Dinner	DINNER
Mission 2: Bridge	OVERPASS
Mission 3: Refrigerator	COOLER
Mission 4: Graveyard	NECROPOLIS
Mission 5: Castle	CITADEL
Mission 6: Tan Base	MOUSE
Mission 7: Revenge	ESCAPE
Mission 8: Desk	ESCRITOIRE
Mission 9: Bed	COT
Mission 10: Plasticville	BLUEBLUES
Mission 11: Toy Shelf	BUYME
Mission 12: Cashier	EXPRESS
Mission 13: Toy Train Town	LITTLEPEOPLE

continued

MISSION	PASSWORD
Mission 14: Rocket Base	NUKEM
Mission 15: Pool Table	EIGHTBALL
Mission 16: Pinball Machine	BLACKKNIGHT

Final Mission

ATV OFFROAD FURY

TOUGHER GAME

Select the Pro-career and enter the name ALLOUTAI when prompted. You'll be sent back to the main menu when entered correctly.

1000CC ATV

Defeat the Pro-Career to earn the 1000cc ATV.

Super ATV

CRAZY TAXI

PUSH BIKE

At the driver select hold L1 + R1, release L1 then R1. Again hold L1 + R1, release and press **X**.

Push Bike

EXPERT MODE

After you choose the time limit, hold L1 + R1 + Start "Expert Mode" will appear in the lower corner at the driver select.

DISABLE ARROWS

After you choose the time limit, hold R1 + Start "No Arrows" will appear in the lower corner at the driver select.

No Arrows

DISABLE DESTINATION

After you choose the time limit, hold L1 + Start "No Destination Mark" will appear in the lower corner at the driver select.

Another Day

ANOTHER DAY MODE

At the driver select press R1 and release, then hold R1 and press X. "Another Day" will appear in the lower corner.

DYNASTY WARRIORS 2

WU CHARACTERS

At the Main Menu press ■, ■, R2, R2, R1, R1, ■, ■. You will hear a sound if entered correctly.

UNLOCK ALL HIDDEN CHARACTERS

At the Main Menu press ■, R1, ■, R2, ■, R2, ■, R1. You will hear a sound if entered correctly.

Choose Sides

FREE MODE
SIDE SELECTION

At the Main Menu press hold ▲ and press R1, L1, L2, R2, R1, L1, L2, R2. You will hear a sound if entered correctly.

OPENING CINEMA EDITOR

At the Main menu press R2, R2, R2, L2, L2, L2, R1, L1. You will hear a sound if entered correctly.

An Opening Edit option will appear in the Options Menu.

GAUNTLET: DARK LEGACY

CHEAT CODES

Enter the following as your name. You can only use one at a time.

EFFECT	CODE
10,000 Gold	10000K
9 Potions And Keys	ALLFUL

Full Load

Pojo the Chicken	EGG911

Pojo the Chicken

Small Enemies	DELTA1

continued

Invincible	INVULN

Invincibility

Invisible	000000
Anti Death	1ANGEL
Full Turbo Meter	PURPLE
Faster	XSPEED
X-Ray	PEEKIN
Reflective shots	REFLEX
3-Way Shot	MENAGE
Supershot	SSHOTS

Supershot

Rapid Fire	QCKSHT

SECRET COSTUMES

Enter the following as your name. Each code is a different costume.

CLASS	COSTUME CODES
Dwarf	ICE600
	NUD069
Jester	KJH105
	PNK666
	STX222
Knight	ARV984
	BAT900
	CSS222
	DARTHC
	DIB626
	KAO292
	RIZ721
	SJB964
	STG333
	TAK118
Valkyrie	AYA555
	CEL721
	TWN300
Warrior	CAS400
	MTN200
	RAT333
Wizard	DES700
	GARM00
	GARM99
	SKY100
	SUM224

GUNGRIFFON BLAZE

12 FUEL AIR BOMBS

Enter "FEA MASTER!" as a pilot name, "Mexico" as a country, and "Female" as the sex.

KENGO: MASTER OF BUSHIDO

PLAY AS A STUDENT

At the character select, hold L1 + L2 + R1 + R2 and select a character.

KNOCKOUT KINGS 2001

UNLOCK OTHER BOXERS

From the main menu select Modes then choose Career. Next choose New and enter in one of the names to unlock the corresponding boxer.

ENTER:	UNLOCK:
MECCA	Ashy Knucks
AUSTIN	Ray Austin
NELSON	Trevor Nelson
JGIAMBI	Jason Giambi
HATCHER	Charles Hatcher
OSUNA	Bernardo Osuna
DEFIAGBN	David Defiagbon
MRBARRY	Barry Sanders
ZITO	Chuck Zito
BOSTICE	David Bostice
DEMART	David DeMartini
BAILEY	Joe Mesi
JBOTTI	John Botti
JRSEAU	Jr Seau
OWNOLAN	Owen Nolan
STEVEF	Steve Francis

MDK2 ARMAGEDDON

KURT IN HIS BOXERS

At the Main Menu, hold L2 + R2 and press ■, ■, ▲, ■.

Nice boxers

Drop Camera

DROP CAMERA

Pause the game, hold L2 + R2 and press ●, X, ●, X. Re-enter the code to return the camera to normal.

INVINCIBILITY

Pause the game, hold L2 + R2 and press Up, Up, Down, Down, Left, Left, Right, Right, ■, ▲, ■, ▲, Select, Start.

NASCAR 2001

BLACK BOX CLASSIC CAR
Win the Short Track Challenge.

BLACK BOX EXOTIC CAR
Win the Half Season.

EA SPORTS CAR
Win the Road Course Challenge.

EA.COM CAR
Win the Superspeedway Shootout on Veteran.

RICHARD PETTY'S CAR
Win a Season on Rookie difficulty.

TREASURE ISLAND TRACK
Win a season on the Veteran difficulty.

NBA HOOPZ

CHEAT CODES

After selecting your team(s), use the ■, **X**, and ● to input the following codes. The first number is the number of times you press ■, the second if for **X** and the third is for ●. After entering the correct number of button presses, press the joystick or d-pad in the noted direction.

For example, for Infinite Turbo you would press ■ three times, **X** once and ● twice. Then press Up. The words Infinite Turbo will appear above the icons.

EFFECT	CODE
No Fouls (Teams must agree)	2-2-2 Right
No Goaltending	4-4-4 Left
No Hotspots (Teams must agree)	3-0-1 Up
Show Hotspot	1-1-0 Down
Infinite Turbo	3-1-2 Up
Granny Shots	1-2-1 Left
Show Shot %	0-1-1 Down
Home Uniform	0-1-4 Right
Away Uniform	0-2-4 Right
ABA Ball	1-1-1 Right
Big Heads	3-0-0 Right
Tiny Heads	3-3-0 Left
Tiny Players	5-4-3 Left
Beach Court	0-2-3 Left
Street Court	3-2-0 Left

Away Jerseys

Tiny Heads on Beach Court

ABA Ball & Big Heads

Big Heads on Street Court

Tiny Players

NBA LIVE 2001

IMPROVE A SUPER STAR'S STATS

From the Main Menu, open the Active Menu. Then select Roster. Choose the Edit Player option and the teams will load if your Create a Player List is empty.

Choose the team and the player that you want to improve and then select the statistic that needs improvement. You can take a star's stats to 99. The screen scrolls down to reveal more stats so don't forget those!

Finally, save the player to access another one.

NHL 2001

PLAY AS "THE HAMMER"

Enter the Rosters menu and select Create Player. Use the name "Hammer" for the player's first name and you will be referred to as "The Hammer" during gameplay.

PLAY AS "ANIMAL"

Enter the Rosters menu and select Create Player. Use the name "Hammer" for the player's first name and you will be referred to as "Animal" during gameplay.

ONI

INVULNERABILITY

Press Select during a game, highlight Help and press L2, L1, L2, ■, ● ■, R3, L3, R3, ●. You should hear a sound if entered correctly.

ONE SHOT KILLS

Press Select during a game, highlight Help and press L2, L1, L2, ■, ●, ■, L3, R3, ●, ■. You should hear a sound if entered correctly.

STRONGER PUNCH

Press Select during a game, highlight Help and press L2, L1, L2, ■, ●, ■, R3, L3, ●, ■. You should hear a sound if entered correctly.

UNLIMITED AMMO

Press Select during a game, highlight Help and press L2, L1, L2, ■, ●, ■, L2, L2, L1, L3. You should hear a sound if entered correctly.

INVISIBLE

Press Select during a game, highlight Help and press L2, L1, L2, ■, ●, ■, L1, R3, L2, L3. You should hear a sound if entered correctly.

Invisible

Level Skip

LEVEL SKIP

Press Select during a game, highlight Help and press L2, L1, L2, ■, ●, ■, L3, R3, L2, L1. You should hear a sound if entered correctly.

CHARACTER SELECT

Press Select during a game, highlight Help and press L2, L1, L2, ■, ●, ■, L2, L2, L2, L2. Continue to press L2 until you find the character you want.

Character Select

Small Character

SMALL CHARACTER

Press Select during a game, highlight Help and press L2, L1, L2, ■, ● ■, R3, L3, R3, ●. You should hear a sound if entered correctly.

BIG CHARACTER

Press Select during a game, highlight Help and press L2, L1, L2, ■, ●, ■, R3, ■, ●, L3. You should hear a sound if entered correctly.

Big Character

Big Heads

BIG HEADS

Press Select during a game, highlight Help and press L2, L1, L2, ■, ●, ■, Start, ■, ●, Start. You should hear a sound if entered correctly.

TOUGHER DIFFICULTY

Press Select during a game, highlight Help and press L2, L1, L2, ■, ●, ■, R3, L3, ●, ■. You should hear a sound if entered correctly.

ONIMUSHA

CLEAR GAME INFORMATION

Upon completion of your first game of ONIMUSHA: WARLORDS, you will be given a letter-grade rank for your performance in the game. This ranking is based upon a combination of three basic elements: the total play time, the total number of souls collected and the number of demons killed. The number of Fluorite

stones collected determines whether secret trailers and mini-games will be unlocked, and adds them as options to the main menu. The number of levels cleared in the Dark Realm Arena are also displayed, but does not affect your overall ranking. The following tables break down ranking into its individual parts, and then show how final ranking is determined.

Ranking Screen

PLAY TIME RANKING

TIME	POINTS
00:00 – 01:00	10
01:01 – 02:00	10
02:01 – 03:00	10
03:01 – 04:00	7
04:01 - 05:00	5
05:00 hours or more	3

TOTAL NUMBER OF SOULS

SOULS	POINTS
34999 or less	3
35000 – 44999	5
45000 – 54999	7
55000 or more	10

NUMBER OF ENEMIES DEFEATED

KILLS	POINTS
399 or less	3
400 – 499	5
500 – 599	7
600 or more	10

FINAL RANKING

RANK	NAME	POINTS
S (Superior)	Oni Musha (Demon)	30*
A	Ara Musha (Wild)	25 - 29
B	Niga Musha (Pain)	18 - 24
C	Hashi Musha (Beginner)	10 - 17
D	Ochi Musha (Sunken)	00 - 09

UNLOCKING BONUSES

FLUORITE STONES	UNLOCKS
00 - 09	Special Trailer
10 - 19	Samanosuke Extra
20	Uni Spirits Mini-game*

*If you collect all 20 the first time, all the bonuses unlock as well.

SUPERIOR RANKING

To achieve an S ranking, you must finish the game in less than 3 hours, kill 600 or more demons and collect 55,000 or more souls. We suggest that you develop your skills, kill every demon you encounter, and keep crossing back and forth through each area until it seems like no more demons are going to show up for now. After reaching new areas, backtrack to previous locations to find new demons. Skip through all the CG cinemas using the START button, and Pause your game by pressing the SELECT button any time you need to refer to the manual or leave the game momentarily. At the end of the game, skip the cinemas before and after the fight with Fortinbras, and also skip the credits and closing shot. These things will all greatly reduce your game time and make it easier to get the required number of kills and souls needed to achieve a Superior ranking. When you do, the **Kaede Extra** becomes available. This is a really cute second costume for Kaede, including little bat wings!

SPECIAL TRAILER

Recording a clear game data, a new menu called "Special Feature" is opened. One of the things that becomes unlocked in this menu is the Special Trailer. This is a two minute preview of the next chapter in the ONIMUSHA saga.

Special Trailer

SAMANOSUKE EXTRA

Extra Costume

Find at least 10 Fluorite stones while playing ONIMUSHA and record a clear game data afterward. The Samanosuke Extra costume will become available. Now you can start up a new game, and a sub menu allows you to choose between Samanosuke's regular costume and this new one.

Our favorite samurai is now fully costumed in a theme-park panda suit, complete with a cute little baby panda tucked into the pouch. If you think this is too funny, wait until you see what the gauntlet looks like! Use the L2 Button to flip the costume's head on and off.

Panda Samanosuke

KAEDE EXTRA

Complete the game with a Superior (S) ranking, and the Kaede Extra costume will become available. Kaede looks very cute in her Chinese princess outfit, complete with flapping bat wings.

Panda & Princess

Princess & Panda

ONI SPIRITS MINI-GAME

Collect all 20 pieces of Fluorite during the game, and this special mini game will be unlocked. "Oni Spirits" is twelve levels of fast paced pot-smashing action, where you must smash the required number of pots before enemies smash them. Samanosuke's life drains as he remains on the sacred ground, and you must smash the required number of pots and collect useful items from the red boxes before you completely run out of life. The game teeters from astoundingly easy to impossibly difficult, so have fun!

Oni Spirits

RAYMAN 2: REVOLUTION

MINI-GAMES

Select Options. Then choose Language. Select Voices and Highlight Raymanian Do not select just highlight it. Now, press and hold:

L1 + R1

And enter:

L2, R2, L2, R2, L2, R2.

If you performed the code correctly you'll be taken immediately to a new menu where you can choose between three new mini-games.

CHEAT MENU

During Gameplay you can pause your game and then select Sound. Now Highlight the Mute Selection. Do not select just highlight it. Now, Press and hold:

L1 + R1

And enter:

L2, R2, L2, R2, L2, R2.

If you did it right you'll see a new menu pop up with cheat options. You can turn them on or off by highlight them an hitting the **X** button. If the cheat is Red, it is turned on. If it is Blue, it is turned off.

SOCCER NAMES

You will have to first enable the "Extra Bonus Mini-Games" cheat and select Baby Soccer. While you play this game you can press and hold:

L1 + R1

And Enter:

L2, R2, L2, R2, L2, R2.

Once you have entered the code the Globox who are playing soccer will have their names displayed above their heads while you play.

RC REVENGE PRO

ALL TRACKS

At the Main Menu press L1, R1, R2, ■, ●.

ALL CARS

At the Main Menu press L1, L2, R1, R2, ●, ■.

SKIP TO NEXT CHAMPIONSHIP

At the Main Menu press L1, R1, R2, L2.

READY 2 RUMBLE BOXING: ROUND 2

ALL CHARACTERS

At the Character select press Left, Left, Right, R2, Left, Right, Right, R1, R1, R2.

All Characters

BIG GLOVES MODE

At the Character Select press ←→↑↓, R1, R2. You will hear a bell ring if done correctly.

CHUBBY MODE

At the Character Select press →→↑↓→, R1, R1, R2. You will hear a bell ring if done correctly.

TOOTHPICK MODE

At the Character Select press →→↑↓→, R1, R2. You will hear a bell ring if done correctly.

ZOMBIE MODE

At the Character Select press ←↑→↓, R1, R1, R2. You will hear a bell ring if done correctly.

RUMBLING RING

Select Afro Thunder. Before the fight begins, press **X**, **■**, **X**, **X**, **●**, **▲** and the screen will shake!

RIDGE RACER V

OPENING CINEMA EFFECTS

During the intro, press:

R1 once: black & white graphics

R1 twice: yellowish graphics

R1 three times: blurred graphics

L1: cycle through these options

SENSITIVITY DISPLAY

While in a race, hold Select until a display pops up in the center of the screen. This will show how demanding you are on your car.

Press Select again to remove the display.

RUMBLE RACING

UNLOCKING CUPS

UNLOCK...	BY WINNING THE GOLD ON...
Rookie Cup 2	Rookie Cup 1
EA Rookie Cup	Rookie Cup 2
Pro Cup 1	EA Rookie Cup
Pro Cup 2	Pro Cup 1
Pro Cup 3	Pro Cup 2
EA Pro Cup	Pro Cup 3
Elite Cup 1	EA Pro Cup
Elite Cup 2	Elite Cup 1
Elite Cup 3	Elite Cup 2
Elite Cup 4	Elite Cup 3
EA Elite Cup	Elite Cup 4
EA Stunt Cup	EA Elite Cup

UNLOCKING TRACKS

UNLOCK...	BY WINNING THE GOLD ON...
So Refined	Rookie Cup 1
Passing Through	Rookie Cup 2
Sun Burn	EA Rookie Cup
Falls Down	Pro Cup 1
The Gauntlet	Pro Cup 2
Touch and Go	Pro Cup 3
Surf and Turf	EA Pro Cup
Coal Cuts	Elite Cup 1
Wild Kingdom	Elite Cup 2
Over Easy	Elite Cup 3
Outer Limits	Elite Cup 4
Circus Minimus	EA Stunt Cup

UNLOCKING VEHICLES

UNLOCK...	BY WINNING THE GOLD ON...
Dragon	Rookie Cup 1
Mandrake	Rookie Cup 2
Maclstrom	EA Rookie Cup
Cataclysm	Pro Cup 1
Escargot	Pro Cup 2
El Diablo	Pro Cup 3
Road Kill	EA Pro Cup
Jolly Roger	Elite Cup 1
Malice	Elite Cup 2
Direwolf	Elite Cup 3
Blue Devil	Elite Cup 4

CUP PASSWORDS

In the Game Options select Password and enter the following. Once you open the Pro Cup 1, you get the Pro Class vehicles and the same with Elite.

PASSWORD	NEW CUP	NEW VEHICLE	NEW TRACK
KOZIEC1PU	Rookie Cup 2	Dragon	So Refined
KZOIEC2PI	EA Rookie Cup	Mandrake	Passing Through

continued

PASSWORD	NEW CUP	NEW VEHICLE	NEW TRACK
OORKIEPUC	Pro Cup 1	Maelstrom	Sun Burn
P1PROC1PU	Pro Cup 2	Cataclysm	Falls Down
Q2PROC2YT	Pro Cup 3	Escargot	The Gauntlet
P3PROC3LM	EA Pro Cup	El Diablo	Touch and Go
AEPPROPUC	Elite Cup 1	Road Kill	Surf and Turf
ILETEC1MB	Elite Cup 2	Jolly Roger	Coal Cuts
ILCTEC2VB	Elite Cup 3	Malice	Wild Kingdom
ILQTEC3PU	Elite Cup 4	Direwolf	Over Easy
LEAITEPUC	EA Elite Cup	Blue Devil	Outer Limits
YEAMPLOWW	EA Stunt Cup	None	None
ZEAGTLUKE	None	None	Circus Minimus

VEHICLE PASSWORDS

VEHICLE	PASSWORD
Cobalt	TLACOBTLA
Revolution	PTOATRTOI
High Roller	HGIROLREL
Stinger	AMHBRAAMH
Buckshot	UBTCKSTOH
Sporticus	OPSRTISUC
Gamecus	BSUIGASUM
Van Itty	VTYANIYTT
Redneck Rocket	KCEROCTEK
Thor	THTORHROT
Road Trip	ABOGOBOGA
Interceptor	CDAAPTNIA
XXS TOMCAT	NALDSHHSD
Vortex	1AREXT1AR

SHADOW OF DESTINY

EXTRA OPTION

Complete the game to access the Extra option at the main menu.

EXTRA ENDING

After completing the game five times and getting all of the Ending Files, you can get a new ending by completing the game one more time.

SILENT SCOPE

TRADE 5 SECONDS FOR 1 LIFE

Pause the game and enter:

▲, ✕, RIGHT, LEFT, RIGHT, LEFT, ●, ✕, RIGHT, LEFT, RIGHT, LEFT, DOWN, DOWN, UP, UP

TRADE 1 LIFE FOR 5 SECONDS

Pause the game and enter:

UP, UP, DOWN, DOWN, LEFT, RIGHT, LEFT, RIGHT, ✕, ●

The following secret codes should all be entered at the Mode Select screen.

HIDDEN MODE

RIGHT, DOWN, RIGHT, ■, UP, ■, ■, ▲, DOWN, RIGHT, DOWN, RIGHT, ■, ▲

NO CROSSHAIRS

RIGHT, RIGHT, RIGHT, ■

NO ENEMY TARGETING

RIGHT, RIGHT, RIGHT, RIGHT, LEFT, DOWN, UP, RIGHT

NO SCOPE MODE

RIGHT, DOWN, RIGHT, ■, RIGHT, DOWN, RIGHT, ■.

ROMANTIC MODE

LEFT, RIGHT, RIGHT, ■, ▲

FAST MODE

DOWN, ▲, UP, ■, ▲, DOWN, RIGHT, DOWN, RIGHT, ■, ▲

MIRROR MODE

LEFT, LEFT, RIGHT, ■, DOWN, DOWN, UP, ▲, UP, RIGHT, DOWN, UP, LEFT, DOWN, ■

SILPHEED: THE LOST PLANET

ALL WEAPONS

Enter GLOIRE as your name.

GLOIRE   *Weapons Galore*

SMUGGLER'S RUN

INVISIBILITY

Pause the game and press R1, L1 (x2), R2, L1 (x2), L2. You will hear a sound. Re-enter the code to disable.

Invisibility

LIGHTER CARS

Pause the game and press L1, R1(x2), L2, R2(x2). You will hear a sound. Re-enter the code to disable.

NO GRAVITY

Pause the game and press R1, R2, R1, R2, Up(x3). You will hear a sound. Re-enter the code to disable.

INCREASE TIME WARP

Pause the game and press R1, L1, L2, R2, Right(x3). You will hear a sound. Re-enter the code to disable.

DECREASE TIME WARP

Pause the game and press R2, L2, L1, R1, Left(x3). You will hear a sound. Re-enter the code to disable.

SSX

RUN WITH YOUR BOARD

At the Options Menu, hold R1 + L1 + R2 + L2 and press ■, ▲, ▲, **X**, ■, ▲, ●, **X**. Start a race and you will run with your board on your back. Repeat code to turn the cheat off.

ALL HINTS

At the Options Menu, hold R1 + L1 + R2 + L2 and press ●, **X**, ●, **X**, ●, **X**,

Running Boarder

●, **X**. Start a race and while loading, it will run through all of the hints. This does take some time. Repeat the code at the Options Menu to turn off.

MAX STATS

At the Options Menu, hold R1 + L1 + R2 + L2 and press **X, X, X, X, X, X, X**, ■. Re-enter to change the stats back.

Max Stats

Open Everything

ALL CHARACTERS, BOARDS, COURSES AND COSTUMES

At the Options Menu, hold R1 + L1 + R2 + L2 and press Down, Left, Up, Right, **X**, ●, ▲, ■. Re-enter the code to disable the code and try to earn everything the fun way.

STAR WARS: STARFIGHTER

Enter the following codes at the codes screen in the Options Menu:

ARTIST'S STORYBOARD

JAMEZ

You will be taken back to the code screen when the slideshow is finished.

CHRISTMAS CINEMA

WOZ

Nym will find a Disco Santa.

JAR JAR MODE

JARJAR

All of the controls will be reversed. Disable this by returning to the option menu and choosing the default game options.

SIMON DAY

SIMON

A picture of the LEC team will be shown singling out a certain Simon.

UNLOCK EXPERIMENTAL N-1 FIGHTER

BLUENSF

Another ship will be added to the list of ships in the Bonus Missions. However, you will not be able to select the ship unless you achieve a Gold rating on every mission after defeating the game, or enter the OVERSEER code.

INVINCIBLE MODE

MINIME

UNLOCK EVERYTHING (ALMOST)

OVERSEER

This will not open multi-player levels.

UNLOCK MULTI-PLAYER MODES

ANDREW

DIRECTOR MODE

DIRECTOR

This will randomly change the camera angles during gameplay. However, the control will be lost. You will be able to press R1 and zoom in occasionally and the Select button to change the camera.

Disable this by returning to the Options Menu and restoring the Default settings.

PROGRAMMER'S HIDDEN MESSAGE

LTDJGD

NO H.U.D. (HEADS UP DISPLAY)

NOHUD

"Bonus Feature Unlocked" will pop up on the codes screen to confirm that you have entered the code correctly.

CHARACTER SKETCHES

HEROES

VIEW THE CREDITS

CREDITS

VIEW THE GALLERY

SHIPS

VIEW PLANET SKETCHES AND MORE

PLANETS

DEFAULT MESSAGE

SHOTS or SIZZLE

BURGER DROID

Enter the DIRECTOR code. Select Fighter Training in the bonus missions and a special Droid Chef will be able to be seen on an asteroid.

DEVELOPMENT TEAM PIC

TEAM

STAR WARS: SUPER BOMBAD RACING

GALAXY CIRCUIT
Finish in the top three on each track.

MIRROR TRACKS
Get a gold medal in the Galaxy Circuit.

DARTH VADER
Get a gold medal in the Galaxy Circuit as Anakin Skywalker.

BOBA FETT
At the main menu press ■, ●, ▲, ●, ■.

AAT
At the main menu press ●, ■, ●, ■.

INFINITE BOOST
At the main menu, press L1, R2, L1, R2, Square, Select.

SPACE FREIGHTER ARENA
At the main menu, press L1, R1, Select, Circle.

CHARACTERS ARE SHARKS
At the main menu, press Up, Right, Down, Left, SELECT.

CHARACTERS ARE KAADUS
At the main menu, press L1, R1, L2, R2.

LANGUAGE SELECT
At the main menu, press the certain buttons to get certain languages:

English - Select, Select, Select, ●

German - Select, Select, Select, L1

Spanish - Select, Select, Select, R1

French - Select, Select, Select, R2

Italian - Select, Select, Select, L2

Jawa - Select, Select, Select, ■

Battle Droid - Select, Select, Select, Up

SUPER BUST-A-MOVE

UNLOCK LEVELS

▲, Left, Right, ▲

An icon will pop up in the top right corner of the screen to confirm that you have unlocked more levels. You will be able to access these in the Arcade mode.

UNLOCK KATZE AND FUNGILA

▲, Right, Left, ▲

An icon will pop up in the top left corner of the screen to confirm that you have unlocked more characters.

SURFING H30

BONUS BOARDS AND RIDERS

Defeat the game on Normal difficulty to unlock six new boards, Tyrone King, Lara Barcella, and Gareos.

Defeat the game on Semi-Pro difficulty to unlock six new boards, Jojo, Morsa and Serena Knox.

Defeat the game on Pro difficulty to unlock five new boards, Largo, Lyco Sassa and Mikey Sands.

Defeat the game on Master difficulty to unlock three new boards and Surfroid.

THE BOUNCER

UNLOCKABLE CHARACTERS

There are a total of 15 characters who you can unlock and use to fight in Versus Mode and Survival Modes. To unlock these characters, you must meet certain conditions, which depends upon the player's progress in Story Mode.

Each character has the following costumes:

- Regular costume worn in Story Mode, available in two to four colors.
- Select an alternate costume by holding the L1 or L2 buttons while selecting a character.

ECHIDNA

To unlock Echidna in Versus and Survival Modes, you must defeat her in Battle 6 onboard the MSD Cargo Train. Her Rank improves each time you defeat her in Story Mode, based on your overall Game Rank.

MUGETSU

To unlock Mugetsu with Mask in Versus and Survival Modes, you must defeat him in Battle 10 of Story Mode in the Hanging Garden area. You can unlock Mugetsu without Mask by defeating him in Battle 24 on the Air-Carrier. His Rank improves each time you defeat him in Extra Games, depending on your overall Game Rank. Each of Mugetsu's forms has different moves and skill levels.

DOMINIQUE CROSS

You can unlock Dominique after all the PD-4 units have been destroyed in the Rocket Tower. Her Rank and Extra Skills available depend upon the player's Game Rank at that time.

PD-4

To unlock PD-4, you must defeat the unit in Battle 21 in the Rocket Tower Basement. Its Rank and Extra Skills are dependent upon your overall Game Rank and are improved each time you defeat it.

KALDEA ORCHID

You can unlock Kaldea in Versus and Survival Modes by defeating her in the Galeos Passageway in Battle 25. Her Rank and Extra Skills are improved each time you fight her, depending upon your overall Game Rank.

DAURAGON C. MIKADO

Because you fight the mind behind Mikado several times in the game, he has four forms that you can unlock for use in Versus and Survival Modes. One-armed Dauragon, who fights with only one hand, is unlocked after defeating him in Battle 11 of Story Mode. Normal Dauragon is the first form of final Boss Dauragon; to unlock him, you must defeat him in Battle 26. You can unlock Overalls Dauragon by winning Battle 27. Lastly, to unlock Shirtless Dauragon, you must clear Story Mode three times.

MASTER WONG LEUNG

You must use either Volt or Kou to infiltrate the Mikado Building and to defeat the Black Panther onboard the Galeos. Then use Sion to defeat Dauragon. During the Epilogue, Sion will flash back to his training with Wong. After defeating Wong, he will appear in Versus and Survival Modes. His Rank and Extra Skills are dependent upon the overall Game Rank of your saved game.

LEANN CALDWELL

You must use Kou to infiltrate the Mikado building and defeat Dauragon, after which Kou will encounter Leann during his Epilogue and be forced to fight her. (See Ending Event Sequence in the "Secrets" section of the **Story Mode** chapter.)

After defeating her in battle, Leann will be unlocked for use in Versus and Survival Modes. Her Rank and Extra Skills available are dependent upon the player's overall Game Rank, as recorded in the saved game.

THEME PARK ROLLER COASTER

EVERYTHING IS FREE

While in the park, enter:

(Left, Down, **X**, ●) x 8

Entering this code eight times in a row can be tough, but take your time and don't make a mistake and everything will be free!

GOLDEN TICKETS

While in the park enter:

(Up, Down, Left, Right, ●, Right, Left, Down, Up, ●) x 4

If you enter this four times in a row, you'll have all of the Golden Tickets that you could want.

TIGER WOODS PGA TOUR 2001

RED SHIRT TIGER

Defeat every game in Play Now. This will increase Tiger's stats.

TIMESPLITTERS

COMPLETE GAME

Pause the game, hold L1 + L2 + R1 + R2 and press ▲ (x4), ■, ■, ●, ▲, X, Start.

INVINCIBLE ENEMIES

Pause the game, select Statistics hold L1 + L2 + R1 + R2 and press Left, Right, Up, Down, ▲, ●, ■, Select. You will hear a sound if entered correctly.

TOP GEAR DARE DEVIL

These secret codes should be entered at the main menu.

PAINT JOB

Down, ■, Down, R1, Right, Right, Up, Left, ●, ●, L2, L1

MOTION BLUR MODE

Up, Left, ●, Down, Right, ■, Up, Down, Left, Right, ●, ■

UNREAL TOURNAMENT

4 PLAYER WITH ILINK

You can play up to 4 player multiplayer with 4 PlayStation 2's and a 4 point fire wire hub. Connect fire wire from each PS 2 to the hub.

Start a multiplayer game, pause the game and press Left, ●, Left, Right, ■, Right. It should say "Waiting For Other Players". Have each person hit Start to join the game.

WILD WILD RACING

SECRET MENU

At the options menu hold ■ and press Up, ●, Down, ●, Left, Right, Left, Right, ●.

TOP SECRET MENU

Enter your name as NORTHEND. This will open a Top Secret Menu in the Secret Menu.

WINBACK: COVERT OPERATIONS

ALL CHARACTERS IN VERSUS MODE

At the title screen press Up, Down, Down, Right, Right, Right, Left, Left, Left, Left. Hold ● and press Start.

All Char's VS.

TRIAL MODE

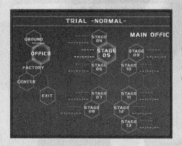

At the title screen press Up, Down, Down, Right, Right, Right, Left, Left, Left, Left. Hold ▲ and press Start.

SUDDEN DEATH MODE

At the title screen press L1, R2, L2, R2, L2, ▲, ●, ▲, ●. Hold L1 and press Start.

MAX POWER MODE (ALL WEAPONS AND INFINITE AMMO)

At the title screen press L1, R2, L2, R2, L2, ▲, ●, ▲, ●. Hold L1 and press Start.

Max Power Mode

ZONE OF THE ENDERS

UNLOCK VERSUS MODE

●, **X**, Right, Left, Right, Left, Down, Down, Up, Up

This will open Versus mode will all of the available characters and environments.

THE GAMES

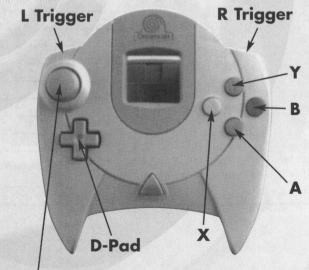

L Trigger

R Trigger

Y

B

A

X

D-Pad

Analog Joystick

CAPCOM VS. SNK

HIDDEN ANIMATIONS

Match the following fighters to get a special intro sequence:

CHARACTER		MATCH UP WITH
Sakura	vs.	Yuri
Cammy	vs.	Vice
Vice	vs.	Rugal
Benimaru	vs.	Any Female Character
Chun-Li	vs.	Mai
Chun-Li	vs.	Yamazaki
Yuri	vs.	Ryo
Ryu	vs.	Ken
Ryu	vs.	Kyo
Ryu	vs.	Ryo
Ryu	vs.	Sagat
Ken	vs.	Terry
Guile	vs.	Rugal
Zangief	vs.	Raiden
Kyo	vs.	Iori
Iori	vs.	M.Bison
Terry	vs.	Yamazaki
Vega	vs.	E.Honda
Vega	vs.	Blanka
Vega	vs.	Zangief
Vega	vs.	Raiden
Vega	vs.	Benimaru
Vega	vs.	Any Female Character
Terry	vs.	Geese
M.Bison	vs.	Geese
M.Bison	vs.	Rugal

CRAZY TAXI

TAXI BIKE

At the Character Select screen, press L Trigger + R Trigger (x3) and then hold L Trigger + R Trigger and press Up.

ANOTHER DAY

At the Character Select screen, hold R Trigger and press A to select your character. The phrase "Another Day" will appear on-screen.

NO ARROWS

Hold Start + R Trigger as the Character Select screen appears. The phrase "No Arrows" will appear on-screen.

NO DESTINATION MARK

Hold Start + L Trigger as the Character Select screen appears. The phrase "No Destination Mark" will appear on-screen.

EXPERT MODE
(NO ARROWS OR DESTINATION MARK)

Hold L Trigger + R Trigger + Start as the Character Select screen appears. The word "EXPERT" will appear on-screen.

DIFFERENT VIEWS AND SPEEDOMETER

During a game, press the Start button on a controller in port three. You can then press A, B or Y on this controller to toggle between views. Press X (x5) for the speedometer. Press X again to turn off the speedometer.

DAVE MIRRA FREESTYLE BMX

Enter PROQUEST mode to enter the following codes:

UNLOCK SLIM JIM

While in the Rider Select Screen, enter:

DOWN, DOWN, LEFT, RIGHT, UP, UP, Y

UNLOCK ALL BIKES

While in the Bike Select Screen, enter:

UP, LEFT, UP, DOWN, UP, RIGHT, LEFT, RIGHT, Y

You will have to do this code for each of the riders.

UNLOCK ALL STYLES

While in the Style Selection Screen, enter:

LEFT, UP, RIGHT, DOWN, LEFT, DOWN, RIGHT, UP, LEFT, Y

You will have to do this code for each of the riders.

UNLOCK ALL LEVELS

While in the Track Select Screen, enter:

LEFT, UP, RIGHT, DOWN, LEFT, DOWN, RIGHT, UP, LEFT, Y

You will have to do this code for each of the riders.

F355 CHALLENGE

HIDDEN COURSES

Hold X + Y at the Options screen to access the passwords option. These passwords are case-sensitive. Enter the following to access the hidden tracks:

Hidden Tracks

Fiorano Track

PASSWORD	COURSE
DaysofThunder	Atlanta
LiebeFrauMilch	Nurburgring
Stars&Stripes	Laguna-Seca
KualaLumpur	Sepang
CinqueValvole	Fiorano

LOONEY TUNES SPACE RACE

Go to the Cheats option in the Options Menu and enter the following secret codes:

UNLOCK	CODE
Porky	YAVARMINT

Th-th-that's Porky

Marvin	REDWAGON

Marvin Martian

ACME 2	MAROON
Mars 2	SCWEWBALL
Off World 1	DURNIDGIT
Off World 2	PALOOKA
Wild West 1	HOGGRAVY
Nebula	MRFUZZY
Galactorama 1	YOIKS

continued

UNLOCK	CODE
Galactorama 2	DODGPARRY
All ACME Events	3LILBOPS

All ACME Events

All Challenges	MOIDALIZE
All Gallery Items	MICHIGANJ

Gallery

Unlimited Turbo	DUCKAMUCK
Mirror Mode	SAMRALPH
No Gags	SUCCOTASH
Everything!	CHEESEFISH

NBA 2K1

CODES

In the Options menu select Codes to enter the following:

CODE	EFFECT
Heliumbrain	Big Heads
Alienbrain	Monster Players
Tvirus	Infected Players
Sohappy	Happy Players
the70'slive	70's Uniforms
Whatamisaying	Crazy Commentary
Betheball	Basketball Camera
Vc	SegaNet, Mo Cap, Sega Sports Teams

NBA HOOPZ

CHEAT CODES

After selecting your team(s), use the X, A, and B buttons to input the following codes. The first number is the number of times you press X, the second is for A and the third is for B. After entering the correct number of button presses, press the joystick or d-pad in the noted direction.

For example, for Infinite Turbo you would press X three times, A once and B twice. Then press Up. The words Infinite Turbo will appear above the icons.

EFFECT	CODE
No Fouls (Teams must agree)	2-2-2 RIGHT
No Goaltending	4-4-4 LEFT
No Hotspots (Teams must agree)	3-0-1 UP
Show Hotspot	1-1-0 DOWN
Infinite Turbo	3-1-2 UP
Granny Shots	1-2-1 LEFT
Show Shot %	0-1-1 DOWN
Home Uniform	0-1-4 RIGHT
Away Uniform	0-2-4 RIGHT
ABA Ball	1-1-1 RIGHT
Big Heads	3-0-0 RIGHT
Tiny Heads	3-3-0 LEFT
Tiny Players	5-4-3 LEFT
Beach Court	0-2-3 LEFT
Street Court	3-2-0 LEFT

NFL QUARTERBACK CLUB 2001

CHEATS

Select Enter Cheat in the Options menu and enter the following. You will hear a sound if entered correctly.

EFFECT	CODE
Large Coin	BGMNY
Smoking Football	HSNFR
Flubber Ball	FLBBR
Big Football	BCHBLL
Large Players	MRSHMLLW
Skinny Players	TTHPCK
Rugby Mode	RGBY
Eight Downs	DBLDWNS
No Fumbles	STCKYBLL
More Fumbles	BTTRFNGRS
More Injuries	HSPTL

PHANTASY STAR ONLINE

Start a new game. While in the character creation mode, enter the following secret codes as your name to gain additional costumes. After the codes are entered, you can rename yourself as you wish. A happy sound will be played if you entered the code correctly.

UNLOCK ALTERNATE COSTUMES

CHARACTER	CODE
Formarl	DNEAOHUHEK
Fonewearl	XSYGSSHEOH
Fonewm	ASUEBHEBUI
Hucast	RUUHANGBRT
Humar	KSKAUDONSU
Hunewearl	MOEUEOSRHUN
Racaseal	NUDNAFJOOH
Racast	MEIAUGHYSN
Ramar	SOUDEGMKSG

QUAKE III ARENA

CONSOLE COMMANDS

Note: The following codes require a Dreamcast Keyboard.

During a game, press ~. This will open the System Window. You will now be able to enter the codes provided.

QUAKE III ARENA COMMANDS

COMMAND	EFFECT
/who	List of players
/help	Display the list of commands
/say	Type a message to everyone
/say1	Message to Player 1
/say2	Message to Player 2
/say3	Message to Player 3
/say4	Message to Player 4
/say_team	Message to team
/tell_attacker	Message to attacker
/tell_target	Message to target
/clear	Clear console

RAYMAN 2: THE GREAT ESCAPE

GLOBOX DISC ACCESS GAME

At the title screen, press Start, then hold the L + R triggers and press B, B, B, B before the screen scrolls all the way down.

Globox Disc

READY 2 RUMBLE BOXING: ROUND 2

ALL CHARACTERS

At the Character select press LEFT, LEFT, RIGHT, L, LEFT, RIGHT, RIGHT, R, R, L.

All Characters

BIG GLOVES MODE

At the Character Select press ← → ↑ ↓, R, L. You will hear a bell ring if done correctly.

CHUBBY MODE

At the Character Select press → → ↑ ↓ →, R, R, L. You will hear a bell ring if done correctly.

ZOMBIE MODE

At the Character Select press ← ↑ → ↓, R, R, L. You will hear a bell ring if done correctly.

TOOTHPICK MODE

At the Character Select press → → ↑ ↓ →, R, L. You will hear a bell ring if done correctly.

RUMBLING RING

Select Afro Thunder. Before the fight begins, press A, X, A, A, B, Y and the screen will shake!

SAMBA DE AMIGO

ALL MUSIC MODE

Select arcade mode, then quickly shake Left Maraca High fifteen times at the height selection screen to unlock all songs. Note: For the standard Dreamcast controller, hold the Left Maraca High button.

RANDOM MODE

Quickly shake Left Maraca Low fifteen times at the difficulty selection screen. Note: For the standard Dreamcast controller, hold the Left Maraca Low button.

SUPER HARD MODE

Quickly shake Left Maraca High fifteen times at the difficulty selection screen. Note: For the standard Dreamcast controller, hold the Left Maraca High button.

SILENT SCOPE

TRADE 5 SECONDS FOR LIFE

Pause the game and enter B, A, RIGHT, LEFT, RIGHT, LEFT, DOWN, DOWN, UP, UP.

TRADE LIFE FOR 5 SECONDS

Pause the game and enter UP, UP, DOWN, DOWN, LEFT, RIGHT, LEFT, RIGHT, A, B.

HIDDEN MODE

At the Mode Select enter RIGHT, DOWN, RIGHT, X, UP, X, X, Y, DOWN, RIGHT, DOWN, RIGHT, X, Y.

NO CROSSHAIRS

At the Mode Select enter RIGHT, RIGHT, RIGHT, X.

NO ENEMY TARGETING

At the Mode Select enter RIGHT, RIGHT, RIGHT, RIGHT, LEFT, DOWN, UP, RIGHT.

NO SCOPE MODE

At the Mode Select enter RIGHT, DOWN, RIGHT, X, RIGHT, DOWN, RIGHT, X.

ROMANTIC MODE

At the Mode Select enter LEFT, RIGHT, RIGHT, X, Y.

FAST MODE

At the Mode Select enter DOWN, Y, UP, X, Y, DOWN, RIGHT, DOWN, RIGHT, X, Y.

MIRROR MODE

At the Mode Select enter LEFT, LEFT, RIGHT, X, DOWN, DOWN, UP, Y, UP, RIGHT, DOWN, UP, LEFT, DOWN, X.

FIRST-PERSON

At the Mode Select enter UP, UP, UP, UP, DOWN, DOWN, DOWN, DOWN.

NIGHT MODE

At the Mode Select enter UP, RIGHT, DOWN, LEFT, UP, X, Y.

SPIDER-MAN

EVERYTHING

In Special select Cheats and enter LEANEST.

Unlock Everything

FULL HEALTH

Enter WEAKNESS as a cheat.

INVULNERABLE

Enter ADMNTIUM as a cheat.

Stick Spidey

PLAY AS STICK SPIDEY

Enter STICKMAN as a cheat.

UNLIMITED WEBBING

Enter GLANDS as a cheat.

CHARACTERS VIEWER

Enter RGSGLLRY as a cheat.

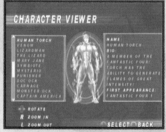

Character Gallery

Level Select

LEVEL SELECT

Enter MME WEB as a cheat.

PULSATING HEAD

Enter EGOTRIP as a cheat.

COMIC COLLECTIONS

Enter FANBOY as a cheat.

Comic Collection

GAME COMIC COVERS

Enter KIRBYFAN as a cheat.

In-Game Comic Covers

EXTRA COSTUMES

Enter the following cheats:

COSTUME	CHEAT
Amazing Bag Man	KICK ME
Ben Reilly	CLUBNOIR
Captain Universe	TRISNTNL
Peter Parker	MRWATSON
Quick Change	SM LVIII
Scarlet Spider	XILRTRNS
Spidey 2099	MIGUELOH
Spidey Unlimited	SYNOPTIC
Symbiote Spidey	SECRTWAR

TEST DRIVE LE MANS

COMPLETE ALL CHAMPIONSHIPS

Enter CARNAGE as your name in Championship Mode

TONY HAWK'S PRO SKATER 2

The following secret codes should be entered at the pause screen while in a game. **Hold the Left Trigger while entering the code.** If the code is entered correctly, you will see the Pause Menu shake.

For secret codes that effect gameplay by altering the environment or the skater, you can disable the option by re-entering the code. For example, if you enter the code for $5000, it won't take the money away again after re-entering the code.

ENVIRONMENTAL EFFECTS

DISCO LIGHTS
DOWN, UP, X, B, UP, LEFT, UP, A

MOON PHYSICS
A, X, LEFT, UP, DOWN, UP, X, Y

DOUBLE MOON PHYSICS
LEFT, UP, LEFT, UP, DOWN, UP, X, Y, LEFT, UP, LEFT, UP, DOWN, UP, X, Y.

JET PACK MODE
UP, UP, UP, UP, A, X, UP, UP, UP, UP, A, X, UP, UP, UP, UP

Controls:

A = Jet Blast on or off

Y = Hover

L = Strafe left

R = Strafe right

PERFECT BALANCE
RIGHT, UP, LEFT, X, RIGHT, UP, X, Y

KID MODE
B, UP, UP, LEFT, LEFT, B, UP, DOWN, X

MIRROR MODE
UP, DOWN, LEFT, RIGHT, Y, A, X, B, UP, DOWN, LEFT, RIGHT, Y, A, X, B

SIM MODE
B, RIGHT, UP, LEFT, Y, B, RIGHT, UP, DOWN

SLO-NIC MODE
B, UP, Y, X, A, Y, B

BLOOD OR NO BLOOD
RIGHT, UP, X, Y

SMOOTH SHADING
DOWN, DOWN, UP, X, Y, UP, RIGHT

WIREFRAME MODE
DOWN, B, RIGHT, UP, X, Y

FASTER SPEED
DOWN, X, Y, RIGHT, UP, B, DOWN, X, Y, RIGHT, UP, B

CAREER ENHANCEMENT

INSTANT $5000
A, DOWN, LEFT, RIGHT, DOWN, LEFT, RIGHT

100,000 POINTS IN COMPETITION
X, B, RIGHT, X, B, RIGHT, X, B, RIGHT

CLEAR ENTIRE GAME WITH CURRENT SKATER
B, LEFT, UP, RIGHT, B, LEFT, UP, RIGHT, A, B, LEFT, UP, RIGHT, B, LEFT, UP, RIGHT

SKIP TO RESTART
X, Y, RIGHT, UP, DOWN, UP, LEFT, X, Y, RIGHT, UP, DOWN, UP, LEFT, B, UP, LEFT, Y

STATS

STATS AT 5
UP, X, Y, UP, DOWN

STATS AT 6
DOWN, X, Y, UP, DOWN

STATS AT 7
LEFT, X, Y, UP, DOWN

STATS AT 8
RIGHT, X, Y, UP, DOWN

STATS AT 9
B, X, Y, UP, DOWN

STATS AT 10
A, Y, B, X, Y, UP, DOWN

STATS AT 13
A, Y, B, A, A, A, X, Y, UP, DOWN

UNLOCK CODES

UNLOCK ALL GAPS

DOWN, UP, LEFT, LEFT, B, LEFT, UP, Y, Y, UP, RIGHT, X, X, UP, A

Trixie will become available to you in the character select screen.

UNLOCK ALL SECRET CHARACTERS

X, B, RIGHT, Y, B, RIGHT, B, Y, RIGHT, X, RIGHT, UP, UP, LEFT, UP, X

UNLOCK EVERY LEVEL

UP, Y, RIGHT, UP, X, Y, RIGHT UP, LEFT, X, X, UP, B, B, UP, RIGHT

UNLOCK EVERYTHING (MASTER CODE!)

This code won't unlock Trixie. You will have to earn her by finding all the gaps or unlocking them all with a code.

A, A, A, X, Y, UP, DOWN, LEFT, UP, X, Y, A, Y, B, A, Y, B.

Once this is entered, end your run.

UNLOCK GYMNASIUM IN SCHOOL LEVEL

Grind the Roll Call! Opunsezmee Rail with about 1:40 on the clock to open the door to the gym.

UNREAL TOURNAMENT

Pause during a game to enter these codes:

LEVEL SKIP

UP, DOWN, LEFT, RIGHT, RIGHT, LEFT

INVINCIBILITY

LEFT, LEFT, RIGHT, RIGHT, DOWN, UP

MAXIMUM AMMUNITION

LEFT, RIGHT, LEFT, RIGHT, RIGHT, LEFT

THE GAMES

NINTENDO 64®

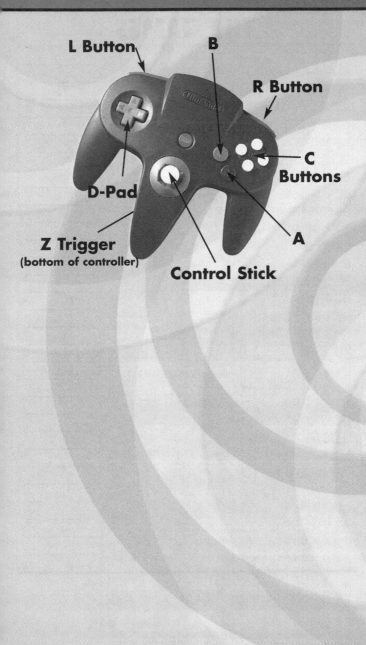

L Button

B

R Button

C Buttons

D-Pad

A

Z Trigger
(bottom of controller)

Control Stick

ALL-STAR BASEBALL 2001

Tom Thumb

Flying Players

TOM THUMB MODE

Enter TOMTHUMB as a code.

FLYING PLAYERS

Enter FLYAWAY as a code.

ALUMINUM BATS

Enter HOLLOWBATS as a code.

BIG BASEBALL

Enter BCHBLKTPTY as a code.

BALL TRAIL MODE

Enter WLDWLDWST as a code.

Big Baseball

No Textures

PARK HAS NO TEXTURES

Enter MYEYES as a code.

NEGATIVE SPACE NO STADIUM AND NO BACKGROUND

Enter WTOTL as a code.

LIZARD TEAM

Select Kaufmann Stadium and hit the Win a Lizard sign in right or left field. Your team should turn into lizards.

Negative Space

ARMY MEN: AIR COMBAT

1-PLAYER CAMPAIGN PASSWORDS

MISSION	CODE
2	Up, Down, Left, Right
3	Up, Down, Left, Up
4	Down, Up, Left, Right
5	Down, Up, Left, Down
6	Down, Up, Right, Down
7	Left, Down, L Button, Up
8	Left, Down, L Button, Down
9	Left, Up, L Button, Down
10	L Button, Up, Left, Down
11	L Button, Up, Left, Up
12	L Button, Up, L button, Down
13	L Button, Down, Up, Left
14	R Button, C-Left, Up, Right
15	C-Down, L Button, Down, Down
16	R Button, C-Left, Right, Up

ARMY MEN: SARGE'S HEROES 2

PLAY AS PLASTRO

Enter PLSTRLVSVG as a code.

MINI MODE

Enter DRVLLVSMM as a code.

Plastro

Tin Soldier

TIN SOLDIER

Enter TNMN as a code.

Vikki

PLAY AS VIKKI

Enter GRNGRLRX as a code.

ALL WEAPONS

Enter GBZRK as a code.

MAX AMMO

Enter SLGFST as a code.

LEVEL PASSWORDS

Enter the following as codes to skip to that level:

LEVEL	CODE
2 Bridge	FLLNGDWN
3 Fridge	GTMLK
4 Freezer	CHLLBB
5 Inside Wall	CLSNGN

continued

LEVEL	CODE
6 Graveyard	DGTHS
7 Castle	FRNKNSTN
8 Tan Base	BDBZ
9 Revenge	LBBCK
10 Desk	DSKJB
11 Bed	GTSLP
12 Town	SMLLVLL
13 Cashier	CHRGT
14 Train	NTBRT
15 Rockets	RDGLR
16 Pool	FSTNLS
17 Pinball	WHSWZRD

ASTEROIDS HYPER 64

CLASSIC ASTEROIDS

Shoot the green object in Zone 1, Level 15 Classic Asteroids should be available at the main menu.

CLASSIC ASTEROIDS, RELENTLESS MODE AND CREDITS

At the Main Menu hold the L Button and enter:

C-Left, C-Right, C-Up, C-Down, A, C-Up, C-Down, C-Left, C-Right, START.

If you entered the code correctly you'll be shown a new menu with Classic Asteroids and Credits on it. To access the Relentless Mode you will have to enter the Single player option.

CHEAT MENU

During gameplay press the START button to pause the game then enter:

C-Left, C-Left, C-Right, C-Right, B, A, C-Up, C-Up, C-Down, C-Down, START.

More options will become available on the pause screen.

BANJO-KAZOOIE

In Treasure Trove Cove, enter the Sandcastle and spell CHEAT by using your Beak Buster on the desired letter. A sound will confirm the entry of the letter. The following cheats will now be available for you. Two things to keep in mind. The first is that no sound will confirm the correct letter. Secondly, ignore the spaces in the phrases…just spell the entire phrase out.

AREA OPENING CHEATS

ACCESS TREASURE TROVE COVE
THIS COMES IN HANDY TO OPEN SOME WHERE SANDY

ACCESS CLANKER'S CAVERN
THERES NOWHERE DANKER THAN IN WITH CLANKER

ACCESS MAD MONSTER MANSION
THE JIGGYS NOW MADE WHOLE INTO THE MANSION YOU CAN STROLL

ACCESS GOBI'S VALLEY
GOBIS JIGGY IS NOW DONE TREK ON IN AND GET SOME SUN

ACCESS RUSTY BUCKET BAY
WHY NOT TAKE A TRIP INSIDE GRUNTYS RUSTY SHIP

ACCESS CLICK CLOCK WOOD
THIS ONES GOOD AS YOU CAN ENTER THE WOOD

ACCESS FREEZEEZY PEAK
THE JIGGYS DONE SO OFF YOU GO INTO FREEZEEZY PEAK AND ITS SNOW

ACCESS BUBBLEGLOOP SWAMP
NOW INTO THE SWAMP YOU CAN STOMP

HIDDEN EGG CHEATS

The Hidden Egg cheats will only work if you have been to the level previously.

REVEAL THE BLUE EGG IN GOBI'S VALLEY BEHIND THE LOCKED GATE IN THE ROCK WALL

A DESERT DOOR OPENS WIDE ANCIENT SECRETS WAIT INSIDE

REVEAL THE PURPLE EGG IN TREASURE TROVE COVE IN SHARKFOOD ISLAND

OUT OF THE SEA IT RISES TO REVEAL MORE SECRET PRIZES

Purple Egg

REVEAL THE ICE KEY IN FREEZEEZY PEAK IN THE ICE CAVE

NOW YOU CAN SEE A NICE ICE KEY WHICH YOU CAN HAVE FOR FREE

REVEAL THE LIGHT BLUE EGG IN GRUNTILDA'S LAIR— YOU'LL FIND IT IN THE CASK MARKED WITH AN X

DONT YOU GO AND TELL HER ABOUT THE SECRET IN HER CELLAR

REVEAL THE GREEN EGG IN MAD MONSTER MANSION IN THE SAME ROOM AS LOGGO THE TOILET

AMIDST THE HAUNTED GLOOM A SECRET IN THE BATHROOM

REVEAL THE YELLOW EGG IN CLICK CLOCK WOOD IN NABNUTS' TREE HOUSE

NOW BANJO WILL BE ABLE TO SEE IT ON NABNUTS TABLE

REVEAL THE RED EGG IN RUSTY BUCKET BAY IN THE CAPTAIN'S CABIN

THIS SECRET YOULL BE GRABBIN IN THE CAPTAINS CABIN

NOTE DOOR CHEATS

These will pop those note doors open without having to find the required notes.

DOOR 2

THESE GO RIGHT ON THROUGH NOTE DOOR TWO

DOOR 3

NOTE DOOR THREE GET IN FOR FREE

DOOR 4

TAKE A TOUR THROUGH NOTE DOOR FOUR

DOOR 5

USE THIS CHEAT NOTE DOOR FIVE IS BEAT

DOOR 6

THIS TRICKS USED TO OPEN NOTE DOOR SIX

DOOR 7

THE SEVENTH NOTE DOOR IS NOW NO MORE

SWITCH AND OBSTACLE CHEATS FOR GRUNTILDA'S LAIR

These will allow you to alter certain obstacles throughout Gruntilda's Lair. Sometimes, the cheat will even remove them completely.

RAISE THE PIPES NEAR CLANKER'S CAVERN

BOTH PIPES ARE THERE TO CLANKERS LAIR

RAISE THE LARGE PIPE NEAR CLANKER'S CAVERN:

YOULL CEASE TO GRIPE WHEN UP GOES A PIPE

UNLOCK THE PATH NEAR CLANKER'S CAVERN THAT LEADS TO THE CLICK CLOCK WOOD PICTURE

ONCE IT SHONE BUT THE LONG TUNNEL GRILLE IS GONE

REVEAL THE PODIUM FOR THE CLICK CLOCK WOOD JIGGY

DONT DESPAIR THE TREE JIGGY PODIUM IS NOW THERE

UNLOCK THE PATH TO THE RUSTY BUCKET BAY PICTURE (OPEN THE GRILL)

THE GRILLE GOES BOOM TO THE SHIP PICTURE ROOM

UNLOCK THE PATH INSIDE THE GIANT WITCH STATUE, NEAR BUBBLEGLOOP SWAMP (OPEN THE GRILL)
SHES AN UGLY BAT SO LETS REMOVE HER GRILLE AND HAT

UNLOCK THE PATH TO THE FREEZEEZY PEAK PICTURE BEHIND THE ICE CUBE
ITS YOUR LUCKY DAY AS THE ICE BALL MELTS AWAY

UNLOCK PASSAGES BLOCKED BY COBWEBS
WEBS STOP YOUR PLAY SO TAKE THEM AWAY

REVEAL A JIGGY IN GRUNTILDA'S STATUE BY SMASHING THE EYE NEAR MAD MONSTER MANSION
GRUNTY WILL CRY NOW YOUVE SMASHED HER EYE

RAISE THE WATER LEVEL NEAR RUSTY BUCKET BAY
UP YOU GO WITHOUT A HITCH UP TO THE WATER LEVEL SWITCH

UNLOCK THE PATH TO THE CRYPT NEAR MAD MONSTER MANSION (REMOVE THE GATE)
YOU WONT HAVE TO WAIT NOW THERES NO CRYPT GATE

REMOVE THE COFFIN LID IN THE CRYPT
THIS SHOULD GET RID OF THE CRYPT COFFIN LID

CRUMBLE ALL BREAKABLE WALLS
THEY CAUSE TROUBLE BUT NOW THEYRE RUBBLE

ACTIVATE SPECIAL PADS
Skip the lesson from Bottles by entering these codes.

ACTIVATE THE FLY PAD
YOU WONT BE SAD NOW YOU CAN USE THE FLY PAD

ACTIVATE THE SHOCK JUMP PAD
YOULL BE GLAD TO SEE THE SHOCK JUMP PAD

EXTRA HEALTH CHEAT

Skip the note-hunt and get that extra health by entering this cheat.

AN ENERGY BAR TO GET YOU FAR

Remember, to enter a code you must first enter the word CHEAT in the Sandcastle.

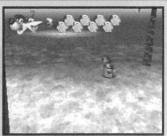

Extra Health

BANJO-TOOIE

CHEATS

Enter the Code Chamber in Mayahem Temple. Stand on the platform in the center and spell CHEATO to access the code entry session.

CODE	EFFECT
JIGGYWIGGYSPECIAL	Level Select
SUPERBANJO	Faster Banjo
SUPERBADDY	Faster enemies
GNIMOH	Homing eggs
SREHTAEF	Doubles feather capacity
SGGE	Doubles egg capacity
NESTKING	Infinite feathers and eggs
KCABYENOH	Energy refills
FOORPLLAF	No damage from falling
XOBEKUJ	Jukebox at Jolly Roger's Lagoon

continued

CODE	EFFECT
JYGGIJTEG	Jiggy signs in Jiggywiggy's Temple
PLAYITAGAINSON	All cinemas in Replay Mode

All Cinemas

JIGGYSCASTLIST	Character Parade

Character Parade

BATTLEZONE: RISE OF THE BLACK DOGS

FREE BUILDINGS

At the Main menu, hold Z and press A, B, A, B.

FREE SATELLITE

At the Main menu, hold Z and press B, C-Left, C-Down, A.

INFINITE AMMO

At the Main menu, hold Z and press L Button, R Button, L Button, R Button.

INFINITE ARMOR

At the Main menu, hold Z and press Up, Right, Down, Left.

UNLOCK ALL LEVELS

At the Main menu, hold Z and press C-Up, C-Right, C-Down, C-Left, Start.

Unlock All Levels

BOMBERMAN 64: THE SECOND ATTACK

MORE CHARACTERS

After finishing Level 5 Challenge, hold Z and press A at the character select.

CARMAGEDDON 64

ALL CARS

Enter your name as CRASHBURN. You should hear applause if entered correctly

CONKER'S BAD FUR DAY

From the Cock and Plucker, select options and then enter Cheats. Now, enter the following codes. The Fire Imp will acknowledge whether you entered a correct cheat or not. Try entering the wrong cheat two times in a row—he'll say something special.

IN-GAME CHEATS

50 LIVES

BOVRILBULLETHOLE

VERY EASY MODE

VERYEASY

EASY MODE

EASY

UNLOCK CHAPTERS IN CHAPTER MODE

UNLOCK BARN BOYS
PRINCEALBERT

UNLOCK BATS TOWER
CLAMPIRATE

UNLOCK SLOPRANOS
ANCHOVYBAY

UNLOCK UGA BUGA
MONKEYSCHIN

UNLOCK SPOOKY
SPANIELSEARS

UNLOCK IT'S WAR
BEELZEBUBSBUM

UNLOCK THE HEIST
CHOCOLATESTARFISH

UNLOCK EVERY CHAPTER AND CUT-SCENE
WELDERSBENCH

MULTIPLAYER CHARACTER CHEATS

UNLOCK CONKER
WELLYTOP

UNLOCK NEO CONKER
EASTEREGGSRUS

UNLOCK GREG THE GRIM REAPER
BILLYMILLROUNDABOUT

UNLOCK SERGEANT AND TEDIZ LEADER
RUSTYSHERIFFSBADGE

UNLOCK ZOMBIES AND VILLAGERS
BEEFCURTAINS

UNLOCK CAVEMAN
EATBOX

UNLOCK WEASEL
CHINDITVICTORY

EXTRA MULTIPLAYER CHEATS

UNLOCK THE FRYING PAN IN THE RACE
DUTCHOVENS

UNLOCK THE BASEBALL BAT IN THE RACE
DRACULASTEABAGS

EXTRA BRUTAL MULTIPLAYER
SPUNKJOCKEY

This is a weird one. Play multiplayer alone in a level that has Katana Swords and Chainsaws. Get one of them and attack the enemy for a cool death animation.

CYBERTIGER WOODS GOLF

PLAY AS LILTIGER

Select Tiger, choose Edit Name, and change it to **Prodigy**.

Liltiger

Marvin

PLAY AS MARVIN THE ALIEN

Select any character, choose Edit Name, and change it to **Ufo**.

PLAY AS KIMMI

Select any character, choose Edit Name, and change it to **Rapper**.

PLAY AS STARR

Select any character, choose Edit Name, and change it to **Retro**.

UNLOCK VOLCANO COURSE

Select any character, choose Edit Name, and change it to **Sthelens**.

Volcano Course

DAIKATANA

ALL WEAPONS CHEAT

At the stage select screen press C-Left, C-Down, C-Right, C-Up, Z, L button, R button, C-Left, C-Down, C-Right, C-Up. A sound will confirm a correct entry.

All Weapons

Stage Select

STAGE SELECT CHEAT

At the stage select screen press C-Up, C-Right, C-Down, C-Left, R button, L button, Z, C-Up, C-Right, C-Down, C-Left. A sound will confirm a correct entry.

DR. MARIO 64

HARD AI IN VS. COMPUTER AND FLASH MODES

Select your opponent by holding L and pressing A. It should change to LV Hard.

Hard AI

Super Hard AI

S-HARD AI IN VS. COMPUTER AND FLASH MODES

Select your opponent by holding L and pressing B. It should change to LV S-Hard.

DUKE NUKEM: ZERO HOUR

CHEAT MENU

At the Press Start screen, press Down, Down, A, Z, Z, Left, A. You'll hear a tone when entered correctly.

1ST PERSON PERSPECTIVE

At the Press Start screen, press Down, Up, L Button, B, Z, Left, C-Up, C-Right, C-Left, Z. You'll hear a tone when entered correctly.

Cheat Menu

FREEZE THROWER WITH UNLIMITED AMMO

At the Press Start screen, press Down, Up, A, L Button, R Button, Z. You'll hear a tone when entered correctly.

UNLIMITED RIFLE AMMO

At the Press Start screen, press C-Up, C-Down, C-Left, C-Right, L Button, R Button. You'll hear a tone when entered correctly.

CHARACTER SET 1

At the Press Start screen, press A, L Button, R Button, Left, B, Down, Up. You'll hear a tone when entered correctly.

Character Set 1

CHARACTER SET 2

At the Press Start screen, press B, A, A, R Button, L Button. You'll hear a tone when entered correctly.

CHARACTER SET 3

At the Press Start screen, press L Button, L Button, Up, Down, R Button, B, A. You'll hear a tone when entered correctly.

Character Set 3

CHARACTER SET 4

At the Press Start screen, press B (x3), R Button, Left, A. You'll hear a tone when entered correctly.

CHARACTER SET 5

At the Press Start screen, press Right, B, Left, L Button, A, Z. You'll hear a tone when entered correctly.

CHARACTER SET 6

At the Press Start screen, press Up, Down, B, A, A, Left. You'll hear a tone when entered correctly.

Character Set 6

EXCITEBIKE 64

ACCESS THE ENTER A CHEAT CODE SCREEN

At the Main menu, hold L Button + C Right + C Down + A.

Cheat Code Screen

BIG HEAD MODE
Enter **BLAHBLAH** as a cheat code.

SMALL HEAD MODE
Enter **PINHEAD** as a cheat code.

BEAT THIS!!
Enter **PATWELLS** as a cheat code.

STUNT BONUS
Enter **SHOWOFF** as a cheat code.

INVISIBLE RIDER
Enter **INVISRIDER** as a cheat code.

MIRROR MODE
Enter **YADAYADA** as a cheat code.

Invisible Rider

NIGHT MODE
Enter **MIDNIGHT** as a cheat code.

ALL STUNTS
Enter **TRICKSTER** as a cheat code.

UNLOCK HILL CLIMB
Finish 1st in the Gold Round of the Amateur Season.

3D EXCITEBIKE
Finish 1st in the Challenge Round of the Pro Season.

UNLOCK ORIGINAL EXCITEBIKE
Finish the Tutorial Mode.

UNLOCK SOCCER
Finish 1st in the Silver Round of the Novice Season.

GEX 3 DEEP COVER GECKO

PASSWORDS

DOOR	PASSWORD
1	DPXMDGVXCVLCG5WFL
2	C2G57FLRDQJV7FBTCN
3	FFY➜SJB5D5HCVJL8DV
4	GFT➜/M9BH56FBLMF2B

ALL REMOTES AND 99 LIVES

Enter the password M758FQRW3J58FQRW4!.

VAULT PASSWORDS

Get the 4 vault keys to play the hidden level. Enter the following at the vault screen.

	PASSWORD
Extra Life	Triangle, Circle, Star, Square, Square, X
8 Hit Paws	Square, Diamond, Triangle, Triangle, Star, Diamond
10 Lives	Square, X, Circle, Circle, Triangle, Square
Invincible	Square, Star, Triangle, Square, Triangle, Diamond
Alfred	Square, X, Triangle, Square, Star, Star
Cuz	Square, Diamond, Square, Square, Triangle, Diamond
Rex	Square, Star, Star, Square, Triangle, Triangle
DracuGex	Star, X, X, Circle, Square, Triangle
Change Timer	Square, Square, Diamond, Circle, X, X
FMV 1	Circle, Triangle, Square, Star, Diamond, Star
FMV 2	Diamond, Star, Square, X, Triangle, Circle
FMV 3	X, Diamond, Star, Triangle, Triangle, Circle
All FMV's	Star, X, X, Circle, Square, Triangle
Debug	Square, Square, Diamond, Circle, X, X (Press Select to Enter)
Quotes	Square, Triangle, X Star, Square, X
Select Level	Square, Circle, Circle, Triangle, X, X

INDIANA JONES AND THE INFERNAL MACHINE

LEVEL SELECT

Enter FORGEOFF or FORGEALL as a Passcode.

Level Select

DEVELOPMENT TEAM PICTURE

Enter CHEESE!! as a Passcode.

Team Pic

EXPERT MODE

Enter REALHARD as a Passcode.

MARIO GOLF

BONUS COURSES

At the Main Menu, highlight the Clubhouse option and press Z + R Button + A. Then enter the following:

CHEAT	CODE
Camp Hyrule, Cup 1	0EQ561G2
Camp Hyrule, Cup 2	5VW68906
Second Camp Hyrule Cup	5VW68906
Nintendo Power Tournament	KPXWN9N3

MARIO STAR COURSE

Open up the first five courses and get 2,200 points.

LEFT-HANDED GOLFER

Press Z or the L Button while selecting a character.

PLAY AS LUIGI

Defeat Luigi in the Get Character Mode.

PLAY AS YOSHI

After accessing Luigi, defeat Yoshi in the Get Character Mode.

PLAY AS SONNY

After accessing Luigi and Yoshi, defeat Sonny in the Get Character Mode.

PLAY AS WARIO

After accessing Luigi, Yoshi and Sonny, defeat Wario in the Get Character Mode.

PLAY AS HARRY

After accessing Luigi, Yoshi, Sonny, and Wario, defeat Harry in the Get Character Mode.

PLAY AS MARIO

After accessing Luigi, Yoshi, Sonny, Wario and Harry, defeat Mario in the Get Character Mode.

PLAY AS BOWSER

After accessing Luigi, Yoshi, Sonny, Wario, Harry and Mario, defeat Bowser in the Get Character Mode.

PLAY AS MAPLE

Earn 50 Birdie Badges in Tournament Mode.

PLAY AS METAL MARIO

Earn 108 Birdie Badges in Tournament Mode.

PLAY AS DONKEY KONG

Earn 30 points in Ring Mode.

MARIO TENNIS

PLAY LEFT-HANDED

Press Z or the L Button while selecting a character.

STAR CHARACTERS

Win the Star Cup with a character to access the star version of that character. Hold the R Button while you select your character.

SPECIAL GAMES

Select Special Games and then Ring Tournament. Enter the following codes to access these special Cups:

CUP	CODE
Bowser Cup	N24K8QN2P
Donkey Kong Cup	MM55MQMMJ
IGN64 Cup	V2UFMPUZM
Luigi Cup	M1C2YQM1W
Mario Cup	A3W5KQA3C
MarioTennis.com Cup	48HWOR482
Nintendo Power Cup	J6M9PQJ6U
Peach Cup	OF9XFQOFR
Blockbuster Cup	ARM6JQARU

continued

Waluigi Cup	LA98JRLAR
Wario Cup	UOUFMPUOM

SHY GUY

Use anybody to win the singles Star Cup.

DONKEY KONG JR.

Use anybody to win the doubles Star Cup.

SUPER MARIO BROS. COURT

Use Mario to win the singles Mushroom Cup.

MARIO AND LUIGI COURT

Use Mario to win the doubles Star Cup.

BABY MARIO AND YOSHI COURT

Use Yoshi to win the singles Mushroom Cup.

DONKEY KONG COURT

Use Donkey Kong to win the singles Mushroom Cup.

Donkey Kong Court

BIRDO AND YOSHI COURT

Use Birdo to win the doubles Star Cup.

WARIO AND WALUIGI COURT

Use Wario to win the doubles Star Cup.

PIRANHA COURT

Win the Piranha Challenge by getting a perfect 50. You can only use this court in the Piranha Challenge.

MICKEY'S SPEEDWAY USA

UNLOCK DEWEY

Place first in each of the first three circuits at the Amateur difficulty level to unlock Dewey as a playable character.

UNLOCK HUEY

Place your Gameboy version of the game into your Transfer Pak. Place your Transfer Pak into your N64 Controller and turn on Mickey's Speedway for the N64. By having your Gameboy version in your Transfer Pak you can now select Huey.

UNLOCK LOUIE

Place first in each of the first three circuits at the Intermediate difficulty level to unlock Louie as a playable character.

UNLOCK VICTORY VEHICLES CIRCUIT

Win each of the first three circuits at the Professional difficulty level to unlock the Victory Vehicles circuit of Yellowstone, Everglades, Malibu and Washington, D.C.

NBA LIVE 2000

GET MICHAEL JORDAN AS A FREE AGENT

Play against Michael Jordan in one-on-one and beat him to unlock him into the free agent's list.

It helps to play a create-a-player character that has an overall ranking of 99

UNLOCK ISAIAH THOMAS

You can unlock Isaiah Thomas by getting 15 steals at the superstar level to unlock him on your roster.

NFL BLITZ 2001

VERSUS CODES

To enter the following codes, the Z button is for the first slot, A Button is for the second slot and the B Button is the third slot. Then end it with a direction on the Control Stick.

EFFECT	CODE
Tournament Mode (in a 2 team game)	1-1-1 Down
Show Field Goal %	0-0-1 Down
Punt hang time meter	0-0-1 Right

Hang-Time Meter

Fast turbo running	0-3-2 Left
Huge head	0-4-0 Up

Huge Head

EFFECT	CODE
Super blitzing	0-4-5 Up
Hide receiver name	1-0-2 Right
Super field goals	1-2-3 Left

Super Field Goals

No punting	1-5-1 Up
No head	3-2-1 Left
Headless team	1-2-3 Right

Headless Team

Big head	2-0-0 Right
Big heads team	2-0-3 Right
Big football	0-5-0 Right
Tiny players team	3-1-0 Right

Tiny Players Team

EFFECT	CODE
No first downs	2-1-0 Up
Allow stepping out-of-bounds	2-1-1 Left
Fast passes	2-5-0 Left
Power-up teammates	2-3-3 Up
Power-up offense	3-1-2 Up
Power-up blockers	3-1-2 Left
Power-up defense	4-2-1 Up
Target Receiver (no highlighting)	3-2-1 Down
Always QB	2-2-2 Left
Always receiver (requires human teammate)	2-2-2 Right
QB/receiver cancel always	3-3-3 Up
No interceptions	3-4-4 Up
No random fumbles	4-2-3 Down
Invisible (no effect)	4-3-3 Up
Turn off stadium	5-0-0 Left

No Stadium

Weather: clear	2-1-2 Left
Weather: snow	5-2-5 Down

The following codes require both teams to agree (enter the same code):

EFFECT	CODE
Smart CPU	3-1-4 Down
No CPU assistance	0-1-2 Down

continued

EFFECT	CODE
Show more field	0-2-1 Right

More Field

Power-up speed	4-0-4 Left
No play selection	1-1-5 Left
Super blitzing	0-4-5 Up
Hyper blitz mode	5-5-5 Up

NFL QUARTERBACK CLUB 2001

BIG FOOTBALL

Enter BCHBLL at the Cheat screen.

FLUBBER BALL

Enter FLBBR at the Cheat screen.

MORE INJURIES

Enter HSPTL at the Cheat screen.

MORE FUMBLES

Enter BTTRFNGRS at the Cheat screen.

RUGBY MODE

Enter RGBY at the Cheat screen.

OGRE BATTLE 64: PERSON OF LORDLY CALIBER

MUSIC MODE

Start a new game and enter your name as MUSIC_ON. This will automatically take you to the Music Mode.

SAN FRANCISCO RUSH 2049

CHEAT MENU

Press Z + R Button + L Button + C-Up + C-Right at the main menu.

Cheat Menu

INVINCIBLE

At the Cheat Menu, highlight Invincible and press C-right, L Button, R Button, R Button, L Button. Then, hold C-left + C-down and press Z.

ALL PARTS

At the Cheat Menu, highlight All Parts, hold L Button + R Button and press Z. Release the buttons, press C-Down, C-Up, C-Left, C-Right, hold L Button + R Button and press Z.

BATTLE PAINT SHOP

At the Cheat Menu, highlight Battle Paint Shop and press Z, Z, Z, C-Down, C-Down, C-Down, C-Left, C-Left, C-Left, C-Right, C-Up, C-Left, C-Down.

SUPER SPEED

At the Cheat Menu, highlight Super Speed, press Z, and hold L Button + R Button and press Z. Release the buttons and press C-Down. Hold L Button + R Button and press C-Down. Release and press C-Up, C-Up, C-Up.

SUPER TIRES

At the Cheat Menu, highlight Super Tires and press Z, Z, Z, L Button, R Button, C-Up, C-Up, C-Left, C-Right, C-Down.

BRAKES

At the Cheat Menu, highlight Brakes and press C-Down, C-Down. Hold L Button + R Button and press C-Up. Press C-Up, C-Up. Hold L Button + R Button and press C-Down.

INVISIBLE TRACK

At the Cheat Menu, highlight Invisible Track and press C-Right, C-Right. Hold L Button + R Button and press C-Left. Press C-Left, C-Left, hold L Button + R Button and press C-Right.

Invisible Track

Invisible Car

INVISIBLE CAR

At the Cheat Menu, highlight Invisible Car and press C-Up, C-Down, C-Left, C-Right, L Button, R Button, Z.

FOG COLOR

At the Cheat Menu, highlight Fog Color, hold C-Up + C-Right and press L Button. Hold C-Down + C-Left and press R Button. Release and press C-Right, C-Left, C-Right, C-Left.

SPIDER-MAN

EVERYTHING
Enter TRUBLEVR at the Cheats Menu.

INVULNERABLE
Enter TURTLE at the Cheats Menu.

FULL HEALTH
Enter HELP ME at the Cheats Menu.

UNLIMITED WEBBING
Enter STICKYSTUF at the Cheats Menu.

LEVEL SELECT
Enter LVLSKIPPER at the Cheats Menu.
You will not unlock new costumes with this cheat on.

SOUND TEST
Enter LISTEN at the Cheats Menu.

COMPLETE GALLERY
Enter WHOSINTGM at the Cheats Menu.

ALL COMIC BOOKS
Enter CLTTHMALL at the Cheats Menu.

ALL GAME COVERS
Enter COV VIEW at the Cheats Menu.

ALL SLIDE SHOWS
Enter SMESTORY at the Cheats Menu.

BEN REILLY COSTUME
Enter DA CLONE at the Cheats Menu.

CAPTAIN UNIVERSE COSTUME
Enter POWCOSMIC at the Cheats Menu.

PETER PARKER COSTUME
Enter MISTERMJ at the Cheats Menu.

QUICK CHANGE SPIDEY COSTUME
Enter GTATNKFST at the Cheats Menu.

SCARLET SPIDEY COSTUME
Enter SPID INRED at the Cheats Menu.

SPIDER-MAN 2099 COSTUME
Enter SPTWOKNN at the Cheats Menu.

SPIDEY UNLIMITED COSTUME
Enter LIMITED ED at the Cheats Menu.

SYMBIOTE SPIDEY COSTUME
Enter SYMBSPID at the Cheats Menu.

STARCRAFT 64

CHEATS

You can access the cheats from the Options Menu.

EXTRA MINERALS AND GAS

In Episode 5, Terran Mission 7, surround the bear in the upper middle section of the map.

FASTER BUILDING

In the first level of the Zerg, save the two hives and proceed down to the corner to find the disc.

TWO PLAYER CO-OP GAME: RESURRECTION

Defeat all 58 missions.

INVINCIBLE UNITS

Defeat the first three episodes.

TECH TREE CHEAT

In Episode 3, Protoss Mission 6, move down and to the right into an open area. Find a message, "sacred ground," at the end of the path. Wait here to get the cheat.

NO FOG OF WAR

In Episode 4, Protoss Mission 3, capture the flag above the starting point.

ALL RESEARCH

In Episode 2, Zerg Mission 5, move Karrigan to the left of the cell with the animals in it.

ALL UPGRADES

In Episode 1, Terran Mission 4, find a man in orange to.

STAR WARS: EPISODE 1 BATTLE FOR NABOO

PASSCODES

HARD MODE
Passcode: NASTYMDE

LEVEL SELECT (WITH SECRET LEVEL)
Passcode: LEC&FIVE

ONE HIT KILLS
Passcode: EWERDEAD

UPGRADED LASERS
Passcode: ADEGAN

MAX STATS
Passcode: OVERLOAD

INFINITE LIVES
Passcode: PATHETIC

ADVANCED SHIELDS
Passcode: DROIDEKA

Level Select

PINK SHIP
Passcode: RUAGIRL?

DEVELOPER COMMENTARY
Passcode: TALKTOME

GALLERY
Passcode: KOOLSTUF

A new option will appear in the options menu. You will now have access to the Art Gallery in the Showroom.

Gallery

MUSIC

Passcode: WAKEUP

You will have access to the Concert Hall in the Showroom. All the in-game music will be available.

Music

Team Pic

TEAM PICTURE

Passcode: LOVEHUTT

SEA SICK MODE

Passcode: DRJEKYLL

The background will bend and warp.

VIEW THE CREDITS

Passcode: MEMEME!

Roll Credits

STUNT RACER 64

I WANT TO BE A MILLIONAIRE!

Key in B, Z, Z, B, Up, C-Down, Z and START on the second Controller during a race. Spend your Regis Philbin-ish moolah on niftier chariots and upgrades.

SKATEBOARDING IS NOT A CRIME

Start a new season and name yourself BUCKYB. A skateboard will be added to your garage, but you'll need to win one race before you can hop aboard it.

MILK TRUCK

Start a new season and name yourself MOOOOO. A milk truck will be added to your garage, but you'll need to win one race before you can drive it. This and the skateboard are two of the game's top vehicles.

BLURRY GLASSES

Start a race. On the second Controller, press B, Left, Up, Right, Right, Right, A, Start, Start, Z, Right, A, Up, Z, C-Down and START.

BIRD'S-EYE VIEW

Start a race. On the second Controller, press Up, Up, Up, A, Left, A, A and A.

VIGILANTE 8: SECOND OFFENSE

Select Game Status from the Options Menu and highlight a character. Press Right Shift + Left Shift to enter the following passwords:

CODE	EFFECT
GO_MONSTER	Big wheels for all cars
NO_GRAVITY	Reduces gravity
HOME_ALONE	Enter a level with no enemies
LONG_MOVIE	Watch all of the movies in a continuous sequence
MIXES_CARS	Enables same cars in multiplayer mode
DRIVE_ONLY	Prevents wheel attachment icons from spawning
BLAST_FIRE	Extra deadly missiles
RAPID_FIRE	Removes the delay between a weapon's fire
UNDER_FIRE	Three enemies attack at once
GO_SLOW_MO	Game goes into slow motion
GO MAX REZ	Activates the Ultra Rez option (needs extra video memory expansion)
GO_RAMMING	Very heavy cars
MORE_SPEED	Faster cars
QUICK PLAY	Enables a random arcade feature for faster action
JACK_IT_UP	Cars are up on stilts

THE GAMES

GAMEBOY®

continued

ABBREV.	WHAT IT MEANS
Left	Left on + Control Pad
Right	Right on + Control Pad
Up	Up on + Control Pad
Down	Down on + Control Pad
Start	Press Start Button
Select	Press Select Button
A	Press A Button
B	Press B Button

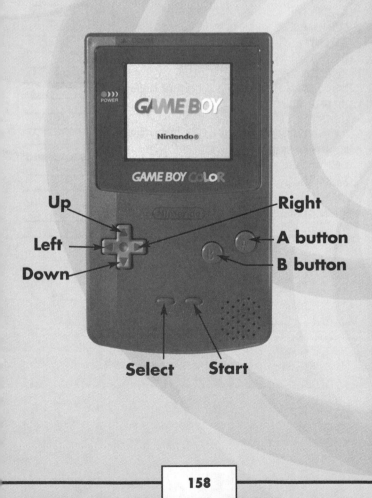

102 DALMATIANS: PUPPIES TO THE RESCUE

GARAGE LEVEL
Enter BONE, BONE, PAWPRINT, TANK

CAFETERIA LEVEL
Enter DOMINO, BONE, KEY, PAW PRINT.

FINAL LEVEL - CRUELLA
At the password entry screen you can enter TOY, BONE, BONE, BONE.

1942

LEVEL 28
At the password entry screen you can enter Medal, Small Plane, Medal, Small Plane

A BUG'S LIFE

PASSWORDS

LEVEL	PASSWORD
1	9LKK
2	BL26
3	5P9K
4	6652
5	BKK2
6	2PLB
7	6562
8	L59B
Bonus	BL26

Level 8

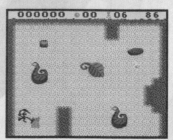
Bonus Level

ACTION MAN

ACCESS ALL LEVELS

Enter 7!B! as a password.

ALADDIN

LEVEL SKIP

Pause the game and press **A, B, B, A, A, B, B, A.**

Level Skip

ARMY MEN

PASSWORDS

LEVEL	PASSWORD
2	Grenade, Machine Gun, Helicopter, Jeep
3	Jeep, Helicopter, Helicopter, Jeep
4	Gun, Grenade, Gun, Grenade

ASTERIX: SEARCH FOR DOGMATIX

PASSWORDS

AREA	PASSWORD
Lutetia	CQPSJ
Massilia	MLSPS
Alexandria	RSFMS
Memphis	TPPGN

Memphis

ASTEROIDS

CHEAT MENU

To enter the Cheat Menu, enter CHEATONX as your password, then press SELECT to enter the menu.

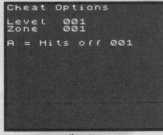

Cheat Menu

CHEAT MENU
Level Select: Up or Down
Zone Select: Left or Right
The A Button toggles Invincibility

PASSWORDS

ZONE	PASSWORD
Zone 2	SPACEVAC
Zone 3	STARSBRN
Zone 4	WORMSIGN
Zone 5	INCOMING

CLASSIC ASTEROIDS

Enter QRTREATR as your password for the original '70s version of the game.

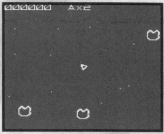

Classic Asteroids

Excalibur

UNLOCK SECRET "EXCALIBUR" SPACESHIP

Enter PROJECTX as your password for the secret ship.

BABE AND FRIENDS

LEVEL PASSWORDS

LEVEL	PASSWORD
02	BOB
03	RN6
04	G5M
05	RM1
06	N6W
07	TYQ

Level 07

BATMAN: CHAOS IN GOTHAM

PASSWORDS

LEVEL	PASSWORD
2	Batman, Batmobile, Batman, Batcycle
3	Batman, Batcycle, Batgirl, Batcycle
4	Batmobile, Batmobile, Batman, Batmobile
5	Batmobile, Batcycle, Batgirl, Batgirl
6	Batcycle, Batcycle, Batman, Batgirl
7	Batcycle, Batgirl, Batgirl, Batman
8	Batgirl, Batcycle, Batman, Batmobile
9	Batgirl, Batgirl, Batmobile, Batcycle

BEATMANIA 2: GACHA MIX

UNLOCK ALL SONGS

Enter the password: YEBISUSAMA

UNLOCK	OTHER SONGS
Friends	MELODIOUS
Rydeen	GROOVY
Ultraman's Song	SUPERCOOL
Genom Screams	WONDERFUL
Unknown	SPLENDID

BILLY BOB'S HUNTIN' N' FISHIN'

HUNT TURKEY AND PIKE

Enter the password: Pig, Boat, Bag, Deer, Bag, Deer

BIONIC COMMANDO

FINAL BOSS

Enter the following password where S=Square, T=Triangle, B=Ball:

	A	B	C	D	E	F
1	S	B	S	S	B	B
2	T	S		T	S	B
3	T	S	B		T	B
4	B	T		B	B	T

RE-EQUIP

Hold **START** and press **A + B**.

GOOD LUCK

Final Boss

BLACK BASS LURE FISHING

FISH BOTH LAKES

At the Password Screen, enter **K** in each space.

```
INPUT PASSWORD
  B C D F G H J
⇨K L M N P Q R
  S T U W X Y Z
  1 2 3 4 5 6 7
  8 9 0 . - OK
KKKK KKKK KKKK KK
```

Both Lakes

BLASTER MASTER: ENEMY BELOW

LEVEL SELECT CODES

LEVEL	CODE
1	E6C3D3KF
2	E6D3D3KG
3	E7C3D3KH
4	E7D3D3KI
5	F6C3D3KQ
6	F6D3D3KR
7	F7C3D3KU
8	F7D3D3KT

BOARDER ZONE

BONUS TRACK

Enter the password: 020971

LEVEL 4 & 5 TRICK ATTACK

Enter the password, 290771. Levels 4 and 5 will now be available in Challenge mode.

BOMBERMAN MAX BLUE: CHAMPION

CHARABOMS	LOCATIONS
Pommy:	1-1
Shell:	1-10
Seadran:	2-2
Panther Fang:	2-10
Beast Pommy:	3-3
Sea Balloon:	3-10
Puteladon:	4-4
Unicornos:	4-9
Iron Squid:	5-8
Animal Pommy:	5-15

CHARABOM COMBINATIONS
Aqua Dragon = Fire + Water
Pommy Dragon = Fire + Electric
Thunder Kong = Earth + Electric
Thunder Shark = Water + Electric
Rock Snakey = Water + Earth

BOMBERMAN MAX RED: CHAMPION

CHARABOM	LOCATIONS
Draco:	1-1
Elephant:	1-10
Marine Eel:	2-2
Knuckle Pommy:	2-10
Big Ox:	3-3
Twin Dragon:	3-10
Sharkin:	4-4
Hammer Pommy:	4-9
Iron Dragon:	5-8
Mecha Kong:	5-15

CHARABOM COMBINATIONS

Aqua Dragon = Fire + Water

Pommy Dragon = Fire + Electric

Thunder Kong = Earth + Electric

Thunder Shark = Water + Electric

Rock Snakey = Water + Earth

Fire Force = Fire + Earth

BUGS BUNNY CRAZY CASTLE 4

PASSWORDS

STAGE	PASSWORD
1-2	RHYO43
1-3	HDYO4?
1-4	7DYO4Z
1-5	KQMO4X
2-1	76504X
2-2	?GPO4Z
2-3	TDPO4X
2-4	KNYS4V
2-5	TQCS34
3-1	1DFS35
3-2	9DFS33
3-3	?Q5S34
4-1	T45S34
4-2	?XP83Z
4-3	RD5S3?
4-4	F4YO34
4-5	34YO32
5-1	WZYO34
5-2	3GYO30
5-3	WNPO3Z
5-4	56303T
5-5	FZMJ24

continued

STAGE	PASSWORD
6-1	5GM03T
6-2	W6WS3V
6-3	P6CS26
7-1	PGCS22
7-2	FQMS24
7-3	M4PS27
7-4	WD5S20
7-5	3DPS22
7-6	H0F02?
8-1	70Y022
8-2	?8Y020
8-3	7SY020
8-4	HJP02Y
8-5	70P02Z
8-6	18P02Y
9-1	PSPJ15
9-2	H0FS17
9-3	72Y814
9-4	KSFS16
9-5	RSFS15
9-6	K0PS25
10-1	RJ5S11
10-2	1B3S1?
10-3	TB3S1Z
10-4	YLW011
10-5	PLW010
10-6	FBC01V
10-7	3BC01S
10-8	W2M01Z
11-1	P0M01X
11-2	W53006
11-3	MSM01T
11-4	F0CS04
11-5	MJCS04
11-6	WSW80Z
11-7	38FS02
11-8	F2M80Z

continued

STAGE	PASSWORD
12-1	PL3S00
12-2	CSPS05
12-3	5V3S0?
12-4	KQR000
12-5	R6RJ0T
12-6	1DT001
12-7	TD900X
12-8	H4KJ?7
13-1	R4KJ?7

BURAI FIGHTER

LEVEL PASSWORDS

LEVEL	PASSWORD		
2	BRFG	NKMR	KDMT
3	KTDC	TCKP	SNNS
4	DRMF	NQTK	KMGT
5	SRSD	MQFH	MSKD

```
        STAGE   5


    PASSWORD   SRSD
```

Level 5

EXTRA CHARACTERS

At the Main Menu, press **Up, Down, Left, Left, Right, Up, A, B, B, A.**

BUZZ LIGHTYEAR OF STAR COMMAND

LEVEL	PASSWORDS
2	BBVBB
3	CVVBB
4	XBVBB
5	YVVBB
6	GBVBB
7	HVVBB
8	3BVBB
9	4VVBB
10	LBVBB
11	MVVBB
12	7BVBB
13	8VVBB

CATWOMAN

PASSWORDS

LEVEL	PASSWORD
Level 2	K6T@1
Level 3	1QT@@
Level 4	KQYXY
Level 5	1@FVQ
Level 6	K@FVP
Level 7	@JFV4
Level 8	KJFZR
Level 9	16TJV

CHASE HQ SECRET POLICE

STAGE SELECT

At the Title Screen, hold **Down + A + B** and press **START**.

Stage Select

CHICKEN RUN

INVISIBILITY

Enter Crown, Bronze, Honor, Valor as a password.

STAGE SKIP

Enter Honor, Valor, Bronze, Silver as a password. Pause the game and press Select to skip to the next stage.

UNLIMITED TIME

Enter Diamond, Honor, Cross, Crown as a password.

PASSWORDS

LEVEL	PASSWORD
2	Bronze, Cross, Crown, Bravery
3	Diamond, Bravery, Honor, Bronze
4	Cross, Bravery, Bronze, Bronze
5	Crown, Diamond, Crown, Honor
6	Valor, Diamond, Cross, Silver

CONKER'S POCKET TALES

RESTORE HEALTH

Save the game when you're low on health. Then load your saved game. Your health should be full.

DAFFY DUCK: THE MARVIN MISSIONS

PASSWORDS

STAGE	PASSWORD	
2	72308	
3	04070	

Level 3

4	82048	

WEAPON SELECT

Defeat ten enemies, pause the game, and enter the following:

Weapon Select

ITEM	CODE
Laser	Up, Up
Big Bullet	Down, Down
Bouncing	Left, Left
Rapid Fire	Right, Right
Health Refill	B, B
No Change	SELECT

DAVE MIRRA FREESTYLE BMX

FULL GAME

Enter the password: R6KZBS7L1CTQMH

Full Game

DONKEY KONG LAND 3

INFINITE LIVES

At the Title Screen, press **Down, Down, Up, Left, Right**.

MATCHING CARD GAME

At the Title Screen, press **Up, Up, Down, Left, Right**. Press **START** to play the game.

Matching Game

DUKE NUKEM

LEVEL SELECT

At the "Press Start" screen, press Left, Right, Up, Up, Down, Up, Right, Left.

INVINCIBILITY

At the "Press Start" screen, press Up, Down, Down, Left, Right, Left, Up, Up. You should hear a noise if you enter the code correctly.

Level Select

EARTHWORM JIM: MENACE 2 THE GALAXY

UNLOCK LEVEL 4

Enter the following passwords at the Password screen:

3bdnkg

3bbbbb

bb3hbl

GRAVEYARD

Enter the following at the password entry screen.

LYBBBB

BBBBBB

BBBBLY

UNLOCK ALL LEVELS

At the password entry screen enter:

EBDNKG

3BBBBB

BB3HBL

ECW: HARDCORE REVOLUTION

RAVEN'S PASSWORDS

Enter in the following passwords to access Raven's career.

WINS	PASSWORD
1 win	qchmhhfg
3 wins	Sfkpkkcj
4 wins	Mgbqbbjc
5 wins	Lhcacckb
6 wins	Pjdsddgf
7 wins	Nkfhfhd
8 wins	Hlqbqqna
9 wins	Gmacaapq
10 wins & TV Title	Knsdsslt
11 wins & TV Title	Jptfttms
12 wins & TV Title	Cqlgllsm
13 wins & TV Title	Brmhmmtl
14 wins & TV Title	Fsnjnnqp
15 wins & TV Title	Dtpkpprn
16 wins & TV Title	Rlglggdh
17 wins & TV Title	Qmhmhhfg

ELEVATOR ACTION

"?" DOOR ITEMS

Enter a "?" Door with the following digits in the hundred spot on your score to get the item:

DIGIT	ITEM
1 or 2	Shotgun
3 or 4	Machinegun
5 or 6	Pistol
6 or 7	Grenade
8 or 9	Heart

EVEL KNIEVEL

UNLOCK SNAKE RIVER CANYON

Enter the password: LASTSTAGE

UNLOCK GRAND FINALE MODE

Enter the password: LEVELS

RESET YOUR GAME

Enter the password: RESET

FIFA 2000

LEVEL	PASSWORDS
2	SDLSNP
3	DCDWTP
4	SPLGZW
5	DQRFKW
6	PSQQLW
7	NBGJVX

FINAL FANTASY LEGEND

SOUND TEST

At the Title Screen, hold **Down + SELECT + A** for about five seconds.

FINAL FANTASY LEGEND II

SOUND TEST

At the Title Screen, hold **SELECT + B + START**.

Sound Test

FORCE 21

MISSION PASSWORDS

MISSION	PASSWORD
2	LXCR
3	PTKL
4	LSGY
5	DUSM

FROGGER

CHEAT MODE

After losing all of your lives, press A, B, Select, Start at the High Score screen.

STOP TRAFFIC AND TURTLES.

Press **A, B, B, Left, Right, Up, B, A** during gameplay. If you do this properly, a traffic light should appear and stop all traffic, and turtles will no longer dive underwater.

GEX: ENTER THE GECKO

ALL REMOTES

Enter the following password by holding the indicated button and pressing the direction at each spot:

B + Down (x20), B + Up, A + Right, A + Left (x2), B + Down (x2), B + Right, A + Right

255 LIVES

To instantly max out your remaining lives, follow these steps:

A: When you have one remaining life, enter a stage with a bottomless pit.

B: Fall down the pit.

C: As the "fall over dead" animation is playing, exit the level through the Pause Menu.

D: Repeat steps A through C and you should have 255 lives. However, you will have to get a Red Remote from *another* stage to be able to receive a valid password.

255 Lives

GEX 3: DEEP POCKET GECKO

MYSTERY TV STATUS

Enter the password: 4BFBBBM329BBBBBBBB

GRAND THEFT AUTO

LEVEL SELECT

Name your character LEVELS or WENDY

HALLOWEEN RACER

ADVANCED LEVEL

To access the advanced level, enter the password 2!!MT9.

HARVEST MOON

FREE EGGS

To get free eggs, buy a chicken and, during the same year, take an egg after it has been laid. Hurl the egg against the wall; it will become stuck in the wall. Use your sickle to cut the egg from the wall and put it in a shipping box. Now cut another egg out the same way. You should be able to acquire nearly 100 eggs from a single one in this fashion.

SELL EGGS AT CHICKEN RATES

Take an egg that one of your chickens has produced and put it into an incubator. Walk to the animal store with it and select "Sell Chicken," but highlight your incubating egg. The store owner will purchase the egg and pay the full price for an actual chicken.

HERCULES

PASSWORDS

LEVEL	PASSWORD
2	B7FG4
3	XTV5P
4	TV5DP
5	FX6NL
6	HGRSV
7	K7DGR
8	FTXCG
9	GSJ4H

Level 9

CREDITS

Enter the password **CRDTS**.

Roll Credits

HOT WHEELS STUNT TRACK DRIVER

UNLOCK ALL CARS AND TRACKS

Enter the password: Down, Left, Up, A, Down, Right

LEVEL PASSWORDS FOR SHADOW JET

LEVEL	PASSWORD
2	Left, Up, Left, Down, Up, A
3	Right, Up, Right, Down, Up, A
4	Up, B, Up, Up, Left, A
5	B, Left, B, Up, Up, Left
6	Down, Left, Up, A, Up, Up
End	Down, Left, Up, A, Down, Right

LEVEL PASSWORDS FOR SLIDE OUT

LEVEL	PASSWORD
2	Down, A, Up, A, B, B
3	Left, B, Left, Right, Down, B
4	Down, B, B, B, Right, Down
5	A, A, Right, Right, B, Down
6	Right, Up, Left, Up, Left, Right
End	Down, Left, Up, A, Down, Right

LEVEL PASSWORDS FOR TOE JAM

LEVEL	PASSWORD
2	B, B, Left, Up, A, B
3	Left, Left, Up, A, Right, Right
4	Left, Left, Up, Left, A, Left
5	Down, Up, Left, Down, Down, A
6	B, B, B, Right, Right, Up
End	Down, Left, Up, A, Down, Right

LEVEL PASSWORDS FOR TWIN MILL

Twin Mill Passwords

LEVEL	PASSWORD
2	Down, Left, B, B, Right, B
3	Up, B, Down, Down, Right, Left
4	Right, Up, Right, B, B, Right
5	Right, Up, Right, Down, A, Right
6	Right, Left, Up, A, Up, Down
End	Down, Left, Up, A, Down, Right

LEVEL PASSWORDS FOR WAY TOO FAST

Way Too Fast Passwords

LEVEL	PASSWORD
2	Right, A, Right, B, Left, Down
3	Down, Right, B, Right, Down, B
4	Right, Right, Down, A, Down, A
5	Up, A, A, Down, Left, Up
6	Left, Up, A, B, B, Right
End	Down, Left, Up, A, Down, Right

INSPECTOR GADGET

PASSWORDS

LEVEL	PASSWORD
2	FH2KBH
3	FM!PQM
4	FRVTLR
5	FWQZ!?

JAMES BOND 007

BONUS GAMES

Enter your name as one of the following:

NAME	GAME
BJACK	Black Jack

Black Jack

BACCR	Baccarat
REDOG	Red Dog

JEREMY MCGRATH SUPERCROSS 2000

UNLOCK 250CC CLASS

Enter the password: SHJBBCGB

THE JUNGLE BOOK

LEVEL SELECT

Enter the password: BMHG

CHEAT MODE

During gameplay, press **SELECT** to access the Options. Select Music/Effects, and play the following sounds in order: 40, 30, 20, 19, 18, 17, 16, 15.

Cheat Mode

KLAX

MINI GAME

Enter the password **Green Alien, Green Alien, Circle, Square.**

KONAMI GAME BOY COLLECTION VOL. 1

LEVEL SELECT FOR CONTRA

To unlock Level Select at the Title Screen, enter: Up, Up, Down, Down, Left, Right, Left, Right, B, A, B, A, START

THE LEGEND OF ZELDA: LINK'S AWAKENING

ALTERNATE MUSIC

Start a new player and enter your name as **ZELDA.**

SAVE YOUR MONEY

To save money on those big purchases, such as the Bow, carry an item to the counter, and as the money starts to drain, immediately press SELECT + START + A + B to go to the Save Menu. Select "Save and Quit," then reload your game. Depending on how fast you were some or even most of your money should be left, and the game won't take what remains.

LITTLE NICKY

UNLOCK A FAR BETTER PLACE

At the password entry screen enter Evilray - Evilray - innerlight - possession

LOONEY TUNES: TWOUBLE

PASSWORDS

Granny's House Pt.1: Dog, Granny, Tweety, Taz, Sylvester

Granny's Cellar Pt.1: Taz, Sylvester, Tweety, Dog, Granny

Garden Pt.1: Sylvester, Tweety, Dog, Taz, Granny

Out in the Streets Pt.1: Dog, Tweety, Taz, Granny, Sylvester

ToyShop Pt.1: Taz, Dog, Tweety, Sylvester, Granny

LUCKY LUKE

PASSWORDS

LEVEL	PASSWORD
1	Luke, Horse, Horse, Old Man, Luke
2	Coyote, Horse, Luke, Old Man, Old Man
3	Old Man, Coyote, Luke, Horse, Coyote
4	Coyote, Horse, Luke, Old Man, Coyote

Level 4

MARIO GOLF

EARN 300 EXPERIENCE

If you find the other three characters, you can earn 300 experience. You can't find the character you are playing as. The following are the locations of each character:

CHARACTER	LOCATION
Sherry	Northernmost part of Tiny Tots
Azalea	Rightmost part of Palm's Putting Grounds
Joe	Leftmost part of Raven Woods
Kid	In the tree by the entrance to the Links Club Putting Range

LEFT-HANDED

Hold SELECT as you choose your character in order to play left-handed. This doesn't work with Sherry, Azalea, Joe, or Kid.

LEVEL UP MUSHROOMS

One is on the bookshelf in the room to the right of the director's room. The second is in the cabinet in the club maker's hut. Look in the bushes to the left of where you arrive at Peach's Castle for the third.

PEACH'S CASTLE COURSE

Win all four tournaments and beat each club's pro.

UNLOCK PUTS, GRACE, TINY, GENE YUSS

Speak to the character in the lounge that you wish to open up. Defeat him or her to play as that character.

UNLOCK WARIO

Defeat the club pros and tournaments.

MEGA MAN 5

ALL POWER-UPS AND ITEMS

Enter the following password:

RRT__

ET__T

_E_RT

TTRRE

TRTRR

All Power-ups and Items

MEN IN BLACK: THE SERIES

FLY

Enter the password **0601**. This should give you an error. During the game, hold **SELECT + Up** to fly. Hold **SELECT + A** to get more firepower.

Error

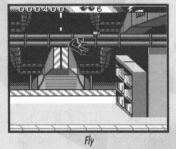

Fly

PASSWORDS

LEVEL	PASSWORD
2	2710
3	1807
4	0309
5	2705
6	3107
Ending	1943

STAGE SKIP

Enter the password **2409**. It should give you an error. While playing, pause the game and press **SELECT** to skip to the next level.

Aliens are on the rampage through the streets of Manhattan...

Stage Skip

MEN IN BLACK: THE SERIES 2

PASSWORDS

LEVEL	PASSWORD
2	MTTH
3	STVN
4	SPDM
5	BTHH
6	BBYH
7	MRLL
8	MMDD

METAL GEAR SOLID

NEW OBJECTIVES

Complete the game on EASY to unlock new objectives for the original levels.

UNLOCK SOUND MODE

Beat all the VR missions: Time Attack and Practice Mode.

MONTEZUMA'S RETURN

UNLIMITED LIVES

Enter the password **ELEPHANT**.

UNLOCK ALL DOORS

Enter the password **SUNSHINE**.

FINAL BOSS

Enter the password **6JYBSPPJ**.

Unlimited Lives

MR. NUTZ

LEVEL PASSWORDS

LEVEL	PASSWORD
2	DDMMNN
3	NNRRGG
4	CCLLRS
5	JJMPPR
6	SWWTCH

Level 6

MULAN

PASSWORDS

LEVEL	PASSWORD
2	JSFPW
3	QGHXB

Level 3

NBA JAM TOURNAMENT EDITION

NO PENALTY FOR GOAL TENDING

On the "Tonight's Match Up" screen, press Right, Up, Down, Right, Down, Up.

EASIER INTERCEPTIONS

On the "Tonight's Match Up" screen, press Left, Left, Left, Left, A, Right.

EASIER THREE-POINTERS

On the "Tonight's Match Up" screen, press Up, Down, Left, Right, Left, Down, Up.

SLIPPERY COURT

On the "Tonight's Match Up" screen, press A, A, A, A, A, Right, Right, Right, Right, Right.

HIGH SHOTS

On the "Tonight's Match Up" screen, press Up, Down, Up, Down, Right, Up, A, A, A, A, Down.

DISPLAY SHOT PERCENTAGE

On the "Tonight's Match Up" screen, press Up, Up, Down, Down, B.

SUPER DUNKS

On the "Tonight's Match Up" screen, press Left, Right, A, B, B, A.

ALWAYS ON FIRE

On the "Tonight's Match Up" screen, press Down, Right, Right, B, A, Left.

NEW ADVENTURES OF MARY KATE AND ASHLEY

LEVEL PASSWORDS

LEVEL	PASSWORD
Volcano Mystery	CBTHPM
Haunted Camp	GMQTCK
Funhouse Mystery	LHDDQJ
Hotel Who-Done-It	MDGKMQ

NFL BLITZ

CHEAT CODES

Enter the following codes at the Match-Up Screen. The first number is how many times you press **START**. The second number is how many times you press **B**. The third number is how many times you press **A**. Then press the direction indicated at the end of the code.

CODE	EFFECT
2,0,2 Right	Brick Field
2,2,2 Right	Night Game
3,2,3 Down	Parking Lot
5,5,1 Up	Predator Mode
0,0,6 Up	Overtime

CODE	EFFECT
5,1,4 Up	Infinite Turbos

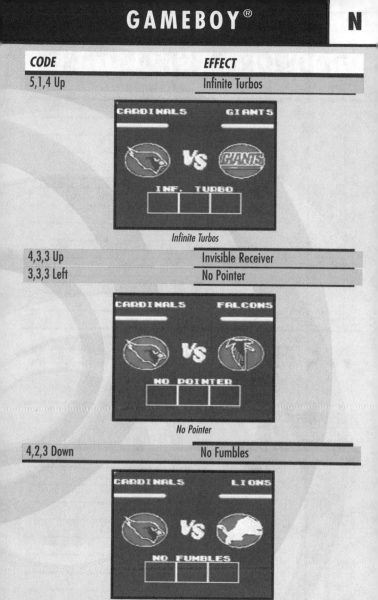

Infinite Turbos

4,3,3 Up	Invisible Receiver
3,3,3 Left	No Pointer

No Pointer

4,2,3 Down	No Fumbles

No Fumbles

PLAY AS EMERYSVILLE ECLIPSE
Enter the password **00606744**.

PLAY AS MIDWAY BLITZERS
Enter the password **06267545**.

ODDWORLD INHABITANTS

LEVEL	PASSWORD
2-0	JCBCM
2-1	JMBCC
2-2	JMCCB
2-3	JPCCD
2-4	JTCCJ
2-5	STCCS
2-6	SBCCT
2-7	TBFCQ
3-1	TBKCL
3-2	TBTCB
3-3	TBTDC
3-4	TBTGF
End	TBTBT

PAC MAN: SPECIAL COLOR EDITION

PASSWORDS

STAGE	PASSWORD
Stage 1:	STR
Stage 2:	HNM
Stage 3:	KST
Stage 4:	TRT
Stage 5:	MYX
Stage 6:	KHL
Stage 7:	RTS
Stage 8:	SKB
Stage 9:	HNT
Stage 10:	SRY
Stage 11:	YSK
Stage 12:	RCF
Stage 13:	HSM

STAGE	PASSWORD
Stage 14:	PWW
Stage 15:	MTN
Stage 16:	TKY
Stage 17:	RGH
Stage 18:	TNS
Stage 19:	YKM
Stage 20:	MWS
Stage 21:	KTY
Stage 22:	TYK
Stage 23:	SMM
Stage 24:	NFL
Stage 25:	SRT
Stage 26:	KKT
Stage 27:	MDD
Stage 28:	CWD
Stage 29:	DRC
Stage 30:	WHT
Stage 31:	FLT
Stage 32:	SKM
Stage 33:	QTN
Stage 34:	SMN
Stage 39:	THD
Stage 40:	RMN
Stage 41:	CNK
Stage 42:	FRB
Stage 43:	MLR
Stage 44:	FRP
Stage 45:	SDB
Stage 46:	BQJ
Stage 47:	VSM
Stage 48:	RDY
Stage 49:	XLP
Stage 50:	WLC
Stage 51:	TMF
Stage 52:	QNS

STAGE	PASSWORD
Stage 53:	GWR
Stage 54:	PLT
Stage 55:	KRW
Stage 56:	HRC
Stage 57:	RPN
Stage 58:	CNT
Stage 59:	BTT
Stage 60:	TMR
Stage 61:	MNS
Stage 62:	SWD
Stage 63:	LDM
Stage 86:	DCR
Stage 97:	PNN

PERFECT DARK

UNLOCK CHEATS IN N64 VERSION

Use your Gameboy version of Perfect Dark to unlock four cheats on your N64 version of Perfect Dark. Use a Transfer Pak and download your information from the Gameboy version to the N64 version. This will make four cheats available. You'll now have the Cloaking Device, Hurricane Fists, the R-Tracker, and every gun in Solo Mode on the N64 version of Perfect Dark!

POCAHONTAS

PASSWORDS

LEVEL	PASSWORD	
2	KPGXH4T8	
3	CMQZB6R1	
4	JWDLF7K5	
5	TGNDX3V9	
6	HFSBD2M6	
7	QZJRL1W4	
8	BPXCV7Z3	
9	SDLFT8G2	

LEVEL	PASSWORD
10	RWHJX9Z5
11	MVNGB4C6
12	KCQTD3W1
13	TBPRG5H8
14	QFCMX2B9
15	VDHKS6L7
16	BNJHZ1R9

POCKET BOMBERMAN

EVERY POWER-UP

To start the game with all power-ups, enter the code **4622**.

ALL ITEMS

Enter the password **5656**.

FIGHT ONLY BOSSES

Enter the password **9437** to play through boss stages back-to-back with all power-ups.

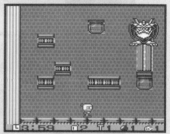

Fight Only Bosses

LEVEL PASSWORDS

FOREST WORLD	PASSWORD
Area 1	7693
Area 2	3905
Area 3	2438
Area 4	8261
Boss	1893

OCEAN WORLD	PASSWORD
Area 1	2805
Area 2	9271
Area 3	1354

Ocean World: Area 3

Area 4	4915
Boss	8649

WIND WORLD	PASSWORD
Area 1	0238
Area 2	5943
Area 3	6045
Area 4	2850
Boss	8146

CLOUD WORLD	PASSWORD
Area 1	9156
Area 2	2715
Area 3	4707
Area 4	7046
Boss	0687

EVIL WORLD	PASSWORD
Area 1	3725
Area 2	0157
Area 3	5826
Area 4	9587
Boss	3752

PRINCE OF PERSIA

PASSWORDS

LEVEL	PASSWORD
2	06769075

Level 2

3	28611065
4	92117015
5	87019105
6	46308135
7	65903195
8	70914195
9	68813685
10	01414654
11	32710744
12	26614774
Jaffar	98119464

Jaffar

continued

LEVEL	PASSWORD
Ending	89012414

Ending

PUZZLE MASTER

PASSWORDS

LEVEL	PASSWORD
1	KING
2	FAIRY
3	WIZARD
4	MOUSE or CHAMPION

NOTE: Enter the word CHEAT as a password to have all of the tools right away.

Level 4

PUZZLED

LEVEL SELECT

At the Password Screen, enter passwords EL001 through EL150, where the number in the code chooses a level between 1 and 150.

R-TYPE DX

DE SOUZA EDITOR

To unlock the De Souza Drawing Editor, you must beat R-Type, R-Type II, and R-Type DX. Then, at the Main Menu, press Right on the + Control Pad, and the De Souza Editor option should appear.

INVULNERABILITY

Beat the DX Game Mode on 10 credits or fewer, then in a non-DX game, press SELECT + A to become indestructible.

LEVEL SKIP

If you've already finished a stage, you can skip it by pressing B while the game is paused.

RAYMAN

ALL LEVELS PASSWORD

Enter CH5G4mSljD as a password.

ACCESS ALL LEVELS

Pause the game and press A, Left, A, Left, A, B, Right, B, Up, B, A, Left, A, Down, .A.

Access All Levels

FILL ENERGY

Pause the game and press B, right, A, Up, B, Left, A, Down, B, Right.

99 Lives

99 LIVES

Pause the game and press A, Right, B, Up, A, Left, B, Down, A, Right, B, Up, A, Left, B.

READY 2 RUMBLE BOXING

FIGHT AS KEMO CLAW

Highlight Arcade Mode and press Left (x3), Right (x3), Left, Right, Left, Right.

FIGHT AS NAT DADDY

Unlock Kemo Claw, highlight Arcade Mode, and press Right (x3), Left (x3), Right, Left, Right, Left.

FIGHT AS DAMIEN BLACK

Unlock Nat Daddy, highlight Arcade Mode, and press Right, Left, Right (x2), Left (x2), Right (x3), Left (x3).

ROAD CHAMPS BXS STUNT BIKING

ALL MODES

Enter QGF7 as a password.

SAN FRANCISCO RUSH 2049

PASSWORDS

TRACK	PASSWORDS
2	MADTOWN
3	FATCITY
4	SFRISCO
5	GASWRKZ
6	SKYWAYZ
7	INDSTRL

TRACK	PASSWORDS
8	NEOCHGO
9	RIPTIDE

Level 9

SHREK: FAIRY TALE FREAKDOWN

PASSWORDS

STAGE	PASSWORD
Village as Thelonius	LRSVGTLXM
Dungeon as Thelonius	YFSVGTLXK
Village as Shrek	SMHTVKCQR
Dungeon as Shrek	TQDFNHGGM
Swamp as Shrek	TFGKWLSJJ
Dark Forest as Shrek	KDNBQGKVY
Bridge as Shrek	KWJPYXCQC
Castle as Shrek	YNNHLBMBY

SIMPSONS: NIGHT OF THE LIVING TREEHOUSE OF HORROR

PASSWORDS

LEVEL	PASSWORD
2	JTWKYTQBBKW
3	TNSLRYSJGWW
4	BXPGCFPYJWB
5	NPKYGBKTFWQ
6	XQRFJWRBTWP

SKATE OR DIE: TOUR DE THRASH

PASSWORDS

LEVEL	PASSWORD
2	GNBF
3	MTGP
4	PVFS
5	FVCH
6	BXHN
7	GFTQ
8	JZWC

SMALL SOLDIERS

PASSWORDS

LEVEL	PASSWORD
4	Archer, Brick, Kip, Chip
5	Kip, Chip, Archer, Brick

SPACE INVADERS

CLASSIC MODE

Enter the password CLSS1281999DBM

Classic Mode

PASSWORDS

LEVEL	PASSWORD
1 Venus	RTJN PBKC X2RJPW
2 Earth	WWYX TC2N QW79VY
3 Mars	?WZ4 VCLN 4W81V?
4 Jupiter	RSSN 3QJ7 8?GJMC
5 Saturn	WSPZ MSO8 N?H8NF
6 Uranus	CV1? QWKG J3X8R5
7 Neptune	HV27 RW1G N3YOR7
8 Pluto	MV7H RCLH S3ZSR9

SPAWN

PASSWORDS

LEVEL	PASSWORD
2	Spawn, Heart, Skull, Heart
3	Heart, Skull, Skull, Flame
4	Heart, Spawn, Skull, Spawn
5	Heart, Skull, Spawn, Spawn
7	Skull, Spawn, Spawn, Heart

SPIDER-MAN

PASSWORDS

GAME LOCATION	PASSWORD
Venom defeated	GVCBF
Lizard defeated	QVCLF
Lab	G-FGN

Lab Level

SPONGEBOB SQUAREPANTS: LEGEND OF THE LOST SPATULA

LEVEL SELECT AND ALL ITEMS

Select Continue and enter D3BVG-M0D3. When you pause the game you should see a Level Select option.

SPY VS. SPY: OPERATION BOOBY TRAP

PASSWORDS

STAGE	PASSWORD
6	ZKP

STAGE	PASSWORD
11	YPT
16	MMD

Stage 16

STAR WARS: EPISODE 1 RACER

A FASTER ANAKIN

Collect every racer and Anakin will be able to hit a maximum speed of 735 mph.

TURBO START

As the "1" fades from your screen press the throttle button. If you get the timing right you'll shoot forward ahead of the pack.

SUPER MARIO BROS. DX

YOU VS. BOO RACE LEVELS

Get 100,000 points in one "normal" game to access these head-to-head stages.

UNLOCK SMB FOR SUPER PLAYERS

Get 300,000 points in one "normal" game to unlock Super Mario Bros. for Super Players. This is the same as the Japanese SMB 2/Super Mario: The Lost Levels, except that Luigi is not available. Instead, Mario has Luigi's higher jumping abilities.

LEVEL SELECT

When you beat the game once, you can select your starting point.

YOSHI EGG FINDER IN CHALLENGE MODE

Once you've found at least one Yoshi Egg, a Yoshi option should appear in the Toy Box. Select it, and a random level's Egg location will be shown. At first, it only shows the screen you should find the egg on, but as you get more eggs, the hints become more detailed.

ALBUM PICTURES

TO GET ALL THE ALBUM PICTURES, DO THE FOLLOWING:

Page 1:	(Top-Left) Fill up the Score Meter in Challenge
	(Top-Right) Get every medal in Challenge
	(Middle) Beat Original Mode
	(Bottom-Left) Beat all the Star Levels in Original
	(Bottom Right) Beat SMB for Super Players
Page 2:	(Top-Left) Get the end-of-level Fireworks
	(Top-Middle) Get a 1-Up Mushroom
	(Top-Right) Find and climb a Bonus Stage Vine
	(Middle-Left) Beat Original 1985 Mode
	(Middle) Save the Princess
	(Middle-Right) Use the link cable to trade High Scores
	(Bottom-Left) Get every Red Coin medal in Challenge
	(Bottom-Middle) Get every High Score medal in Challenge
	(Bottom-Right) Get every Yoshi Egg in Challenge
Page 3:	(Top-Left) Kill a Little Goomba
	(Top-Middle) Kill a Bloober
	(Top-Right) Kill Lakitu
	(Middle-Left) Kill a Cheep Cheep
	(Middle) Kill a Hammer Brother
	(Middle-Right) Kill a Bullet Bill
	(Bottom-Left) Kill a Koopa Troopa
	(Bottom-Middle) Kill a Spiny
	(Bottom-Right) Kill a Buzzy Beetle
Page 4:	(Top-Left) Kill Bowser in World 1 with fireballs
	(Top-Right) Kill Bowser in World 2 with fireballs
	(Bottom-Left) Kill Bowser in World 3 with fireballs
	(Bottom-Right) Kill Bowser in World 4 with fireballs
Page 5:	(Top-Left) Kill Bowser in World 5 with fireballs
	(Top-Right) Kill Bowser in World 6 with fireballs
	(Bottom-Left) Kill Bowser in World 7 with fireballs
	(Bottom-Right) Kill Bowser in World 8 with fireballs

SURVIVAL KIDS

MINI GAMES

Fishing Game: Grab the big rock near the main river. Use the rock where you see fish.

Big Berry Game: First, get a monkey. Now, go to the big berry tree after the river. Use the monkey to play the game.

Egg Catcher Game: Go to the north of the desert with the monkey.

TARZAN

LEVEL PASSWORDS

LEVEL	COMBO
2-1	4-2-3-4
3-1	1-1-5-6
4-1	2-3-7-4
5-1	7-7-3-1
6-1	6-5-4-7

The numbers above refer to the symbols below.

TAZMANIAN DEVIL: MUNCHING MADNESS

LEVEL PASSWORDS

WHAT GOES HERE?	
BLGNGJPDFFTJ	Unlocks China Level
LMBPBKTFKDPK	Unlocks Switzerland Level

TEST DRIVE 6

UNLOCK CARS

Win the Mega Cup and unlock: BMW V12 LMR

PANOZ ROADSTER

You can select them at the "purchase car" screen.

UNLOCK THE MEGA CUP

Win all of the other tournaments to unlock the Mega Cup.

TETRIS DX

WALL-CRAWLING BLOCKS

A bug in Tetris DX allows you to push the "irregular" blocks (not 4-bars or squares) back up the wall. Hold Left or Right until the piece is pressing against the wall. Continue to hold the direction and quickly, repeatedly rotate the piece by pressing the A Button for the left wall and the B Button for the right wall. The block will "climb" up the wall slowly.

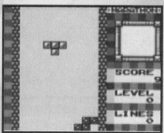

Wall Crawling Blocks

TONY HAWK'S PRO SKATER 2

ALL BOARDS AND LEVELS OPEN

Enter B58LPTGBBBBV as a password.

TOONSYLVANIA

PASSWORDS

LEVEL	PASSWORD
3	4F627
4	XVJRL
5	NMVN3

TOP GEAR POCKET

ALL CARS AND COURSES

Enter the password **YQXW_H**.

ALL GOLD TROPHIES

Enter the password **YQX_%Z**.

Nine Cars and Six Tracks

Enter the password **TWX+%Z** to get a head start that's not quite as big as than the codes above.

All Cars and Courses

TOY STORY 2

SCENE	PASSWORD
2	PBPP
3	BJWJ
4	PJBW
5	WBPP
7	JBPJ
9	JJWW
10	PBWJ
11	BPWW

Level 11

End	WWWW

TUROK 3: SHADOW OF OBLIVION

UNLIMITED AMMUNITION

Enter ZXLCPMZ at the Password Screen.

Unlimited Ammo

UNLIMITED LIVES

Enter FJVHDCK at the Password Screen.

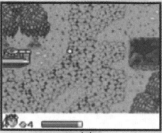

Level Skip

SKIP LEVEL

Enter XCDSDFS at the Password Screen.

EASY PASSWORDS

LEVEL	PASSWORD
2	SDFLMSF
3	DVLFDZM
4	VFDSGPD
5	CSDJKFD

MEDIUM PASSWORDS

LEVEL	PASSWORD
2	VLXCZVF
3	DPSDCVX
4	ZMGFSCM
5	HWKLFYS

HARD PASSWORDS

LEVEL	PASSWORD
2	CJSDPSF
3	CMSDKCD
4	SPFPWLD
5	TPDFQGB

ULTIMATE PAINTBALL

PASSWORDS

LEVEL	PASSWORD
2	9GSMJY2K
3	16FWJJET
4	1B5WJWTO
5	130WJBOY
6	CXXWJROB
7	C3SWJXIA
8	665WJQIU
9	9ZOCJTAK

V-RALLY CHAMPIONSHIP EDITION

PASSWORDS IN ARCADE MODE

DIFFICULTY	PASSWORD
Medium	FAST
Hard	FOOD

Hard Difficulty

WACKY RACES

ALL DRIVERS AND TRACKS

Enter MUTTLEY as a password.

All Drivers and Tracks

WARIO LAND: SUPER MARIO LAND 3

DEBUG MODE

Pause the game and press **SELECT 16 times**. A box should appear on the lives. Hold **B** and press **Left or Right** to select a number to change. Press **Up or Down** to change the number.

Debug Mode

WORMS: ARMAGEDDON

LEVEL PASSWORDS

LEVEL	PASSWORD
Jungle	Pink worm, Banana bomb, Skeletal worm, Pink worm
Cheese	Pink worm, Banana bomb, Blue worm, Dynamite
Medical	Skeletal worm, Blue worm, Banana bomb, Banana bomb
Desert	Red worm, Pink worm, Skeletal worm, Blue worm
Tools	Banana bomb, Pink worm, Pink worm, Blue worm
Egypt	Skeletal worm, Pink worm, Red worm, Banana worm
Hell	Pink worm, Blue worm, Red worm, Dynamite
Tree-hut	Red worm, Skeletal worm, Dynamite, Blue worm

LEVEL	PASSWORD
Garden	Banana bomb, Red worm, Skeletal worm, Dynamite
Snow	Dynamite, Pink worm, Blue worm, Blue worm
Constyrd	Pink worm, Pink worm, Banana bomb, Banana bomb
Pirate	Dynamite, Blue worm, Dynamite, Skeletal worm
Fruit	Skeletal worm, Red worm, Banana bomb, Skeletal worm
Alien	Dynamite, Blue worm, Red worm, Red worm
Circuit	Red worm, Dynamite, Dynamite, Dynamite
Medieval	Blue worm, Dynamite, Skeletal worm, Blue worm

WWF ATTITUDE

JARRETT PASSWORDS

OPPONENT	PASSWORD
Triple H	LGJCRMHG
Shamrock	PKHDSNJK
Val Venis	NJGFTPKJ
Steve Austin	RCFGLQBC
Gangrel	QBDHMRCB
The Rock	TFCJNSDF
Road Dogg	SDBKPTFD
Mankind	CRTLGBQR
Sable	BQSMHCRQ
Kane	FTRNJDST
Goldust	DSQPKFTS
X Pac	HMPQBGLM
Bossman	GLNRCHML

STONE COLD STEVE AUSTIN PASSWORDS

OPPONENT	PASSWORD
Gangrel	CBFPCQJC
Sable	BCDNBRKB
J Jarrett	FDCMFSGF
Undertaker	RQTKRBNR
Road Dogg	QRSJQCPQ

continued

OPPONENT	PASSWORD
The Rock	TSRHTDLT
Bossman	STQGSFMS
Goldust	MLPFMGSM
Taka	LMNDLHTL
Al Snow	PNMCPJQP
Billy Gunn	NPLBNKRN
Val Venis	HQKTHLDH
Edge	GRJSGMFG
X-Pac	KSHRKNBK

THE ROCK CAREER MODE PASSWORDS

VICTORIES	OPPONENT	PASSWORD
1	Road Dogg	GHKRCSCG
2	Taka	KJGSDRDK
3	Triple H	JKHPFRFJ
4	Bossman	CBDQGNGC
5	Godfather	BCFRHPHB
6	Shamrock	ZFDBSJLJF
7	Austin	DFCTKMKD
8	Edge	RQSBLJLR
9	Val Venis	QRTCMKMQ
10	Al Snow	TSQDNGNT
11	X-Pac	STRFPHPS
12	Billy Gunn	MLNGQDQM
15	Kane	NPMKTCTN
16	Mankind	HQJLBSBH
17	Goldust	GRKMCTCG
18	Gangrel	KSGNDQDK

PASSWORDS

EDGE

RANK	PASSWORD	RANK	PASSWORD
01	SHTPLMJG	10	HSGBEDRT
02	BJQLPNHK	11	GTHCDFQS

RANK	PASSWORD	RANK	PASSWORD
03	QKRMNPGJ	12	FLDJHGPM
04	PBNSRQEC	13	DMFKGHNL
05	NCPTQRDB	14	CNBGKJMP
06	MDLQTSCF	15	BPCHJKLM
07	LFMRSTDD	16	TQSNMLKH
08	KQJDCBTR	17	SRTPLMJG
09	JRKFBCSQ	18	RSQLPNHK

GANGREL

RANK	PASSWORD	RANK	PASSWORD
01	TPSTPTHK	10	GLHGBGSQ
02	QLRQLQJG	11	HMGHCHTR
03	RMQRMRKH	12	NJPNSNBD
04	DSFDJDLN	13	PKNPTPCF
05	FTDFKFMP	14	LGMLQLDB
06	BQCBGBNL	15	MHLMRMFC
07	CRBCHCPM	16	SDTSNSGJ
08	JNKJDJQS	17	TFSTPTHK
09	KPJKFKRT	18	QRRQLQJG

GODFATHER

RANK	PASSWORD	RANK	PASSWORD
01	NGHNGDHG	10	CTSCTMST
02	MKJMKCJK	11	BSTBSLTS
03	LJKLJBKJ	12	KMLKMTLM
04	TCBTCKBC	13	JLMJLSML
05	SBCSBJCB	14	HPNHPRNP
06	RFDRFHDF	15	GNPGNQPN
07	QDFQDGFD	16	PRGPHFGH
08	FRQFRPQR	17	NQHNGDHG
09	DQRDQNRQ	18	MTJMKCJK

KANE

RANK	PASSWORD	RANK	PASSWORD
01	???	10	RPQPTJTT
02	JBKBGRGG	11	QNRNSKSS
03	GDHDKSKK	12	PRNRMBMM
04	FHDHCLCC	13	NQPQLCLL
05	DGFGBMBB	14	MTLTPDPP
06	CKBKFNFF	15	LSMSNFNN
07	BJCJDPDD	16	KMJCHQHH
08	TMSMRGRR	17	JLKBGRGG
09	SLTLQHQQ	18	HPGFKSKK

SABLE

RANK	PASSWORD	RANK	PASSWORD
01	???	10	BRLHCPML
02	QCGMAKHG	11	FSPJDLNP
03	TDKNSGJK	12	DTNKFMPN
04	SFJPTHKJ	13	RLHLQJGH
05	MGCQLDBC	14	FSNNFNQP
06	NKDTPCFD	15	DTPPDPRN
07	HLRBGSQP	16	RLGGRGDH
08	GMQCHTRQ	17	QMHHQHFG
09	JPSFKRTS	18	TNJJTJBK

TAKA MICHINOKU

RANK	PASSWORD	RANK	PASSWORD
01	DHJRMMGG	10	MSRJDDTT
02	CJHSNNKK	11	LTQKFFSS
03	BKGTPPJJ	12	TLPBGGMM
04	KBFLQQCC	13	SMNCHHLL
05	JCDMRRBB	14	RNMDJJPP
06	HDCNSSFF	15	QPLFKKNN
07	GFBPTTDD	16	FQKQLLHH
08	PQTGBBRR	17	DRJRMMGG
09	MRSHCCQQ	18	CSHSNNKK

THE UNDERTAKER

RANK	PASSWORD	RANK	PASSWORD
01	SGKTCRHG	10	HTQGNJST
02	RKGQDSJK	11	GSRHPKTS
03	QJHRFTKJ	12	FMNDQBLM
04	PCDNGLBC	13	DLPFRCML
05	NBFPHMCB	14	CPLBSDNP
06	MFBLJNDF	15	BNMCTFPN
07	LDCMKPFD	16	TRJSBQGH
08	KRSJLGQR	17	SQKTCRHG
09	JQTKMHRQ	18	RTGQDSJK

X-PAC

RANK	PASSWORD	RANK	PASSWORD
01	SCJPCHDG	10	GPQCTPNS
02	RDHLDJFK	11	FQPJQLRM
03	QFGMFKDJ	12	DRNKRMOL
04	PGFSGBHC	13	CSMGSNTP
05	NHDTHCGB	14	BTLHATPS
06	MJCQJDKF	15	TLKNBGCH
07	LKBRKFJD	16	SMJPCHBG
08	KLTDLQMR	17	RNHLDJFK
09	HNRBNSPT		

PLAYSTATION LEGAL STUFF

DAVE MIRRA FREESTYLE BMX™ © 2000 Acclaim Entertainment, Inc. All rights Reserved.

F355 CHALLENGE™ **PASSIONE ROSSA** Original Game © SEGA ENTERPRISES, LTD., 1999. © SEGA ENTERPRISES, LTD./CRI 2000/ Developed by AM2 of CRI. All Rights Reserved.

LOONEY TUNES SPACE RACE © 2000 Infogrames. All Rights Reserved.

NBA 2K1 © 2000 SEGA ENTERPRISES, LTD. All Rights Reserved.

NBA HOOPZ © Midway Home Entertainment, Inc. All Rights Reserved.

NFL QUARTERBACK CLUB 2001 © 2001 Acclaim Entertainment, Inc. Acclaim is a registered trademark of Acclaim Entertainment, Inc. All Rights Reserved.

PHANTASY STAR™ **ONLINE** © Sega/Sonic Team 2000.

QUAKE III ARENA® © 1999-2000 Id Software, Inc. All rights reserved. Quake III Arena® for the Sega Dreamcast developed by Raster Productions LLC.

RAYMAN 2: THE GREAT ESCAPE © 2000 Ubi Soft, Inc.

READY 2 RUMBLE BOXING ©1999 Midway Home Entertainment Inc. All rights reserved. Likeness of Michael Buffer and the READY TO RUMBLE registered trademark used under license from Buffer Partnership (www.letsrumble.com). All character names are trademarks of Midway Home Entertainment Inc. MIDWAY is a trademark of Midway Games Inc.

SILENT SCOPE © 1999, 2000 KONAMI. All Rights Reserved.

SPIDER-MAN & Marvel ™ & © 2001 Marvel Characters, Inc. © 2001 Activision, Inc. and its affiliates. All Rights Reserved.

TEST DRIVES LEMANS © 2000 Infogrames Entertainment S.A. All rights reserved.

TONY HAWK'S PRO SKATER 2 © 1999, 2000 Activision, Inc. All rights reserved.

UNREAL TOURNAMENT © 2001 Epic Games, Inc. Developed by Secret Level Games. Published by Infogrames.

NINTENDO 64 LEGAL STUFF

Nintendo 64® is a registered trademark of Nintendo of America Inc. ™, ®, and the "N" Logo are trademarks of Nintendo of America Inc. All rights reserved.

ALL-STAR BASEBALL 2001 ©2000 Acclaim Entertainment, Inc. All rights reserved.

ARMY MEN: AIR COMBAT © 2000 The 3DO Company. All Rights Reserved.

ARMY MEN SARGE'S HEROES 2 © 2000 The 3DO Company. All rights reserved.

ASTEROIDS HYPER 64 © Crave Entertainment. All Rights Reserved.

BANJO-KAZOOIE © 2000 Nintendo/Rare. Game by Rare. Rareware logo is a trademark of Rare. All Rights Reserved.

BANJO-TOOIE © 2000 Nintendo/Rare. Game by Rare. Rareware logo is a trademark of Rare. All Rights Reserved.

BATTLEZONE: RISE OF THE BLACK DOGS ©2000 Activision, Inc. All rights reserved. Battlezone is a trademark of and ©2000 Atari Interactive, Inc., a Hasbro company.

BOMBERMAN 64: THE SECOND ATTACK Published by Vatical Entertainment and developed by Hudson Soft.

CARMAGGEDON 64 Published by Titus and developed by Software Creations.

CONKER'S BAD FUR DAY © 2000 Nintendo/Rare. Game by Rare. Rareware logo is a trademark of Rare. All Rights Reserved.

CYBERTIGER ©2000 Electronic Arts, Inc. All rights reserved.

DAIKATANA © 1997-2000 Ion Storm. L.P. All rights reserved.

DR. MARIO 64 © 2001 Nintendo

DUKE NUKEM: ZERO HOUR ©1996 3D Realms, GT Interactive Software.

EXCITEBIKE 64 © 2000 Nintendo

GEX 3: DEEP COVER GECKO © Crave Entertainment, Inc. All Rights Reserved.

INDIANA JONES AND THE INFERNAL MACHINE ™ © Lucasfilm Ltd. All Rights Reserved.

MARIO GOLF ©1999 Nintendo/Camelot.

MARIO TENNIS © 2000 Nintendo/Camelot.

MICKEY'S SPEEDWAY USA © 2001 Nintendo/Rare. Game by Rare. Rareware logo is a trademark of Rare. All Rights Reserved.

NBA LIVE 2000 © 2000 Electronic Arts, Inc. All Rights Reserved.

NFL BLITZ 2001 © 2000 Midway Amusement Games LLC. All rights reserved.

trademark of Atlus U.S.A.,Inc. ©1998 1999 2000 2001 ATLUS. All rights reserved.

NFL QUARTERBACK CLUB 2001™ 2000 The NFL Quarterback Club is a trademark of the National Football League. © 1999 NFLP. © 1999 Acclaim Entertainment, Inc. All Rights Reserved.

OGRE BATTLE 64: PERSON OF LORDLY CALIBER © 2000 Atlus U.S.A., Inc. Atlus is a registered **SAN FRANCISCO RUSH 2049** is a trademark of Midway Games West Inc. Distributed by Midway Home Entertainment Inc. under license.

SPIDER-MAN Marvel Comics, Spider-Man: ™ & © 2001 Marvel Characters, Inc. All rights reserved. Activision is a registered trademark of Activision, Inc. © 2000 Activision, Inc. All rights reserved.

STARCRAFT 64 © Nintendo 2000. Developed by Blizzard and Mass Media. All Rights Reserved.

STAR WARS: EPISODE I BATTLE FOR NABOO © 2000 LucasArts Entertainment Co., LLC. All Rights Reserved.

STUNT RACER 64 © 1999 by Boss Game Studios, Inc. All rights reserved.

VIGILANTE 8: 2ND OFFENSE is a trademark of Activision, Inc. ©1999 Activision, Inc. All Rights Reserved.

GAME BOY LEGAL STUFF
Game Boy® is a registered trademark of Nintendo of America, Inc.

102 DALMATIONS: PUPPIES TO THE RESCUE Published by Activision, Inc. Developed by Digital Extremes. All rights reserved.

1942 Published by Capcom and developed by Digital Eclipse. All rights reserved.

A BUG'S LIFE ©1998 Disney. All rights reserved. ©1998 THQ. Inc. THQ is a registered trademark of THQ, Inc.

ACTION MAN Published by THQ Inc. and developed by Natsume. All rights reserved.

ALADDIN ©1993 The Walt Disney Company ©1994 Virgin Interactive Entertainment. All rights reserved.

ARMY MEN Published by 3DO and developed by Digital Eclipse. All rights reserved.

ASTERIX: SEARCH FOR DOGMATIX Published by Infogrames and developed by Rebellion. All rights reserved.

ASTEROIDS Published by Activision, Inc. and developed by Syrox. All rights reserved.

BABE AND FRIENDS Published by Crave and developed by IMS Productions. All rights reserved.

BATMAN: CHAOS IN GOTHAM © 2000 Ubi Soft Entertainment, Inc. BATMAN and all related characters, names and indicia are trademarks of DC Comics © 2000. All rights reserved.

BEAT MANIA 2: GACHA MIX © 2000 Konami. Konami is a registered trademark of Konami Co., Ltd. All rights reserved.

BILLY BOB'S HUNTIN' N' FISHIN' © 2000 Midway Home Entertainment Inc. All rights reserved.

BIONIC COMMANDO ©1992 Capcom. All rights reserved.

BLACK BASS LURE FISHING© Starfish, Inc. All rights reserved.

BLASTER MASTER: ENEMY BELOW Published by Sunsoft. All rights reserved.

BOARDER ZONE ™ & © 2000 Infogrames. Boarder Zone and Infogrames are trademarks or registered trademarks of Infogrames North America, Inc.

BOMBERMAN MAX BLUE: CHAMPION/RED: CHALLENGER Developed by Judson. Published by Vatical Entertainment. All rights reserved.

BUGS BUNNY CRAZY CASTLE 4 Published and developed by Kemco. All rights reserved.

BUST-A-MOVE 4 ©1999 Taito Corporation. All rights reserved.

BUZZ LIGHTYEAR OF STAR COMMAND © Disney/Pixar. Activision is a registered trademark of Activision, Inc. © 2000 Activision, Inc. All rights reserved.

CATWOMAN Published by Vatical Entertainment and developed by Kemco. All rights reserved.

CHASE HQ SECRET POLICE Published by Metro 3D. All rights reserved.

CHICKEN RUN Published by THQ and developed by Blitz Games. All rights reserved.

CONKER'S POCKET TALES Developed by Rare. Published by Nintendo. All rights reserved.

DAFFY DUCK: THE MARVIN MISSIONS Looney Tunes, characters, names, and all related indicia are trademarks of Warner Bros. ©1994 Sunsoft. All rights reserved.

DAVE MIRRA FREESTYLE BMX™ © 2000 Acclaim Entertainment, Inc. All rights Reserved.

DONKEY KONG LAND 3 ©1995-1997 Nintendo All rights reserved.

DUKE NUKEM Developed by Torus Games. Published by GT Interactive. All rights reserved.

EARTHWORM JUM: MENACE 2 THE GALAXY
Developed by IMS. Published by Crave Entertainment.
All rights reserved.

ECW HARDCORE REVOLUTION Published by
Acclaim and developed by Crawfish Interactive. All
rights reserved.

EVEL KNIEVEL Developed by Tarantula Studios.
Published by Take 2 Interactive. All rights reserved.

FIFA 2000 Published by THQ and developed by
Tiertex Design Studios. All rights reserved.

FINAL FANTASY LEGEND ©1989 Square Soft.
Licensed by Nintendo. All rights reserved.

FINAL FANTASY LEGEND II ©1991 Square Co.,
Ltd. All rights reserved. Final Fantasy® and
Squaresoft® are registered trademarks of Square Co.,
Ltd. All rights reserved.

FORCE 21 Published by Ubi Soft and developed by
Red Storm. All rights reserved.

FROGGER ™ Frogger is a trademark of Hasbro. All
rights reserved.

GEX: ENTER THE GECKO ™ ©Crystal Dynamics All
rights reserved. Published by Crave Entertainment
©1998 Crave Entertainment.

GEX 3: DEEP POCKET GECKO Developed by IMS.
Published by Eidos Interactive. All rights reserved.

GRAND THEFT AUTO Developed by Tarantula.
Published by RockStar. All rights reserved.

HERCULES ©1997 The Walt Disney Company All
rights reserved. ©1997 THQ Inc.

HOT WHEELS STUNT TRACK DRIVER Published
by Mattel Interactive and developed by Lucky Chicken.
All rights reserved.

INSPECTOR GADGET Published by Ubi Soft and
developed by Light and Shadow Productions. All rights
reserved.

JAMES BOND 007 © Nintendo/Rare. ©1962,
1995 Danjaq, LLC. & U.A.C. All rights reserved. Game
published and distributed by Nintendo. All rights
reserved.

JEREMY MCGRATH SUPERCROSS 2000
Published by Acclaim and developed by M4 Ltd. All
rights reserved.

THE JUNGLE BOOK Published by Ubi Soft. All rights
reserved.

KLAX ©1990 Hudson Soft. ©Atari Games Corp.
©Tengen Inc. ©Tengen Ltd. All rights reserved.

KONAMI'S GAME BOY COLLECTION VOL. 1
Published and developed by Konami. All rights
reserved.

THE LEGEND OF ZELDA: LINK'S AWAKENING
©1993,1998 Nintendo. All rights reserved.

LITTLE NICKY Published by Ubi Soft and developed
by Digital Eclipse. All rights reserved.

LOONEY TUNES: TWOUBLE © Infogames. All
rights reserved.

LUCKY LUKE Developed by Fernando Velez.
Published by Infogrames. All rights reserved.

MARIO GOLF © Nintendo. All rights reserved.

MEGA MAN 5 © Capcom Co., Ltd. 1994. All rights
reserved.

BMEN IN BLACK: THE SERIES ™ ©1998
Columbia Pictures industries, Inc. & Adelaide
Productions, Inc. All rights reserved. Trademark: MEN
IN BLACK™ Columbia Pictures Industries, Inc. Published
by Crave Entertainment, Inc. ©1998 Crave
Entertainment, Inc.

METAL GEAR SOLID is a trademark of Konami Co.,
Ltd. Konami is a registered trademark of Konami Co.,
Ltd. All rights reserved.

MONTEZUMA'S RETURN ©1997, 1998 Utopia
Technologies. All rights reserved.

MR. NUTZ Developed by Planet Interactive.
Published by Infogrames. All rights reserved.

MULAN ©1998 Disney. All rights reserved. ©1998
THQ. Inc.

NBA JAM TOURNAMENT EDITION Published by
Acclaim. All rights reserved.

**NEW ADVENTURES OF MARY KATE AND ASH-
LEY** Published by Acclaim and developed by Crawfish
Interactive. All rights reserved.

NFL BLITZ ©1997 Midway Games Inc. All rights
reserved. BLITZ and MIDWAY are trademarks of
Midway Games Inc. ©1997 NFLP.

ODDWORLD INHABITANTS Published by GT
Interactive and developed by Saffire. All rights
reserved.

PAC MAN: SPECIAL COLOR EDITION Published
and developed by Namco. All rights reserved.

PERFECT DARK ™ & © Rare. All rights reserved.

POCAHONTAS © 1996 Disney Interactive. All rights
reserved.

PRINCE OF PERSIA ©1991 Virgin Games, Inc.
©1989, 1991 Broderbund Software, Inc. Jordan
Mechner. All Rights Reserved. Prince of Persia is a registered trademark of Broderbund Software, Inc.

PUZZLE MASTER Developed and published by Metro
3D. All rights reserved.

R-TYPE DX © 1991 IREM Corporation. Developed by
B.I.T.S. All rights reserved.

RAYMAN © 1995 Ubi Soft Entertainment, Inc. All
rights reserved.